Adam Taor

You wouldn't want Adam looking after you if you were sick, but he'd happily write about it. Adam is a writer who decided soon after qualifying as a doctor that medicine wasn't for him. So he put an ad in the paper saying he wanted a job and ended up a journalist, writing for publications in Australia, Europe and North America. This book germinated out of a column he wrote for *The Weekend Australian*. Nowadays he's head of copy at a Sydney advertising agency and excels at table football (foosball). Adam lives in Rozelle with two cats, Bones and Halo. Email worm_on_my_eyeball@hotmail.com if you want to say hello to them (or even Adam).

Douglas Holgate

Douglas is a freelance illustrator based in Melbourne, Australia. He has work published in Europe, the US and Australia by the likes of Random House, Simon and Schuster, *The New Yorker* magazine and Image Comics. His palatial grounds are open to the public 10 am – 5:30 pm, Monday through Friday. Closed public holidays. He has two cats.

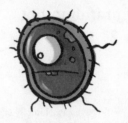

THERE'S A WORM ON MY EYEBALL!

The alien zoo of germs, worms and lurgies that could be living inside you

DR ADAM TAOR

ILLUSTRATED BY DOUGLAS HOLGATE

RANDOM HOUSE AUSTRALIA

To everyone with the courage to be stupid.
A.T.

For my grandmother . . . may you never be afflicted by
chapter 23.
D.H.

Random House Australia Pty Ltd
Level 3,100 Pacific Highway, North Sydney NSW 2060
www.randomhouse.com.au

Sydney   New York   Toronto
London   Auckland   Johannesburg

First published by Random House Australia in 2007

National Library of Australia
Cataloguing-in-Publication Entry

    Taor, Adam.
    There's a worm on my eyeball.

    For primary school children.
    ISBN 978 1 74166 213 9.

    1. Body, Human – Juvenile humor.
    I. Holgate, Douglas. II. Title.

    612.00207

Fart facts on page 31 based on information found in *Wind Breaks: Coming to
terms with wind* by Bolind, T. and Stanton, R., published by Allen & Unwin.

Cover illustration by Douglas Holgate
Cover design by Wideopen Media
Internal design and typesetting by Wideopen Media
Printed and bound by Griffin Press, South Australia

10 9 8 7 6 5 4 3

Contents

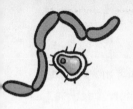

Introduction

Finding the Alien in You!

Prepare yourself for a big bug shock: you are not actually who you think you are! You thought you were a human being, didn't you? You know, the type of living thing that has a head, two arms and two legs . . . and farts, and burps, and picks its nose, and watches TV, and daydreams cool and crazy things, and reads brilliant books on parasitic pests (frequently all at the same time). But this way of looking at yourself is only a small part of the truth, because the mega microbial reality is that much of you isn't human at all: **it's alien!**

That's right – you are more bug than you are Betty or Bill, more alien than you are Arthur or Martha. Cell for cell, there are more bacteria, viruses, fungi and other alien bugs in you than there are cells that are human. In other words, if you counted all the cells in your body, there'd be far more bug ones than human ones. **Spooky!**

What do you think of that, Alien Boys and Girls? And to prove that you're actually an alien bug freak, here are some amazing facts about you (and your poo):

- Inside our intestines – the place where hamburgers become poo patties, Thai noodles turn into turd doodles and fizzy drinks foam into farts that stink – there are hundreds and hundreds of different species of bacteria. **Our guts are chock full of micro-organisms.** And they have a great time living in our body, usually doing us little harm at all.

- If you collected all the bugs in our guts – just the bugs – they'd weigh about one kilogram. That's roughly the same weight as 16 Mars bars. I told you your intestines were *choc* full of bugs!

- It's thought that we have about 100,000,000,000,000 bacteria (that's 100 *trillion*) just in our intestines! If you shared out all of the bacteria living in your guts among everyone in the world, each person would get about 15,000. So, if you're stuck on what to give your family and friends next festive season, why not give the gift of bacteria?

Welcome to Bugsville (pop. 1 gazillion)

Wherever your body is exposed to the outside world, microbes like to get down and dirty. Your skin and your guts are high on the bugs' list of ideal spots to hang out. Your guts may be on the *inside* of you, but, if you think about it, the digestive tract is just a long tube that runs from your mouth to your bum, so the inside of the tube is actually full of stuff from the outside world: food. And bacteria is found in some of the food we eat (and the water we drink and the thumbs we suck . . .) Amazingly, there are roughly 10 billion bacteria in our mouth and 1 trillion on our skin.

If you want to imagine just how many bugs live on your body, have a look at this diagram. It shows the number of bacteria on just one square centimetre of different bits of your skin. And remember, a square centimetre isn't very large at all.

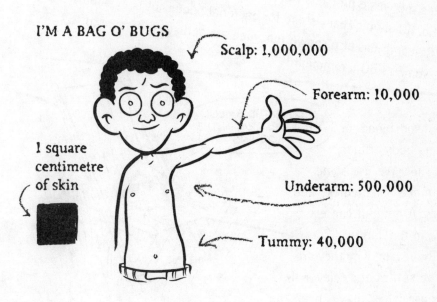

I'M A BAG O' BUGS

Scalp: 1,000,000

Forearm: 10,000

1 square centimetre of skin

Underarm: 500,000

Tummy: 40,000

So it seems all you really are, at least in the microscopic scheme of things, is a nice, warm home for gazillions of grateful guzzling bugs.

Microbial masters of the universe

Bugs are brilliant survivors – that's one reason why they can have so many special powers. Some bugs swim quite fast with propeller-like tails. Others lie sleeping in the earth for years and years before waking and infecting us, while some die quickly if they find themselves outside of their preferred habitat. Some spread in the air, others in

A stink that is truly 'the pits'

Body odour, aka BO, is gross, but the even grosser truth is that the foul whiff actually comes from bacteria that hang out in our armpits. They feed on secretions from glands in our underarms. It's the waste products from their meal that make the nasty pong. So, BO should really stand for bacterial odour not body odour! Research has also shown that men are actually *attracted* to women's BO – mmmmm!

water or blood or other body fluids, like snot. We use some to make medicines and foods. A handful can even glow in the dark!

> I LOVE THE SMELL OF UNDERARM IN THE MORNING

The reason why they are so versatile and clever is because they have been on Earth for an extraordinarily long time, which means they have had lots of practice getting good at what they do best – **stayin' alive**. When I say 'an extraordinarily long time', what I really mean is a 'longer-than-our-brains-can-cope-with' sort of time. You see, bugs – germs, microbes, whatever you want to call them – have lived on Earth *much* longer than humans.

So how long is an EXTRAORDINARILY long time? Bacteria, a very common type of germ, have been around for more than 3.5 billion years. That's about 3,499,999,990 years more ancient than you! If your brain isn't big enough to fit such a monster number in, here's a way of getting an idea of how long a billion years is: roughly a billion *minutes* ago Jesus was alive. About a billion *hours* ago it was the Stone Age and primitive humans were happily doing their primitive thing. A billion *days* ago our ape-like ancestors were busily getting up to monkey business on the plains of Africa. And a billion *months* ago dinosaurs were dodging asteroids and getting stuck in tar pits where they turned into fossils for us to find and put in museums.

So, over the ages, bugs have become very good at overcoming the obstacles that life puts up in front of them. There are bugs that thrive in brain-burningly hot places, and there are microbes that feel just fine in mind-numbingly cold climes. Some germs need oxygen to stay alive, while others get by without it altogether. Some bugs make us ill, while many are quite harmless. And **others even live inside us** and help keep us healthy!

That helps explain why bugs are so common; they thrive everywhere – in us, in the air, in the water, in rocks and in the soil. And just how common they are is almost impossible for our little brains to comprehend.

Get this: scientists in America once worked out that there are about 5,000,000,000,000,000,000,000,000,000,000 bacteria living on Earth! Compare that crazy number to the total number of people living on the planet, which was just a measly 6,544,294,987 on 15 September 2006. In fact, there are more bacteria living right now, than the number of people who have ever lived or ever *will* live on Earth.

You are pond life (well, almost)

Because bugs are very common and very adaptable, they are often more different from each other than they are alike, and that's part of the secret to their success.

Just how different they are is illustrated in this scummy story. There is a type of microbe called a paramecium (pa-ruh-me-see-um) that lives in the water, especially in the gooey, slimy scum that sometimes sits on the surface of ponds. A paramecium is a simple thing: it's made of just one small cell, perhaps 0.0001 metres long, and is a footprint-shaped blob. So, with all due respect to the humble paramecium, it's not going to win a beauty contest or a Nobel Prize or a gold medal in Olympic swimming, is it?

What could we possibly have in common with a little blob of living goo?
We (as in you, me, teachers, criminals, lawyers, footy players and other human beings) may all be different, but, if you think about it, we're really not *that* different. We all breathe the same air, eat pretty much the same food, are comfy in roughly the same temperature and have roughly the same shaped bodies, with insides that work in pretty much exactly the same way. And our genes (the genetic stuff that makes us what we are, not our trousers) are all very nearly the same. Certainly we are a million miles (sorry, a BILLION miles) away from being related to a scum-loving, single-celled piece of pond life with a funny name like paramecium. Like I said, you won't see a paramecium swimming at the Olympics.

THERE'S A LITTLE BIT OF *ME* IN PARAMECIUM

But it turns out that, on one level, we are much more like a paramecium than we realise. If you look at our genes, you'll see that we have more in common with this single-celled swimming blob than some bacteria have in common with other bacteria!

In other words, our genes and a paramecium's genes are quite similar to each other, compared with how different one bacteria's genes can be from another bacteria's genes!

This book is overflowing with all sorts of over-the-top organisms: **brilliant bacteria**, **villainous viruses** and a **humungous fungus** or two. But they aren't the only types of bug you'll come across here on your journey from the shallow end of lurgy-ness to the depths of deadliness. There is also a smattering of other creatures, like weird and wonderful worms, jumping fleas, fully sick ticks, not nice lice and mites that'll give you quite a fright.

Bacteria fact-eria

FACT 1: Bacteria are made of just one cell.

FACT 2: They are usually about 0.000001 metres long. So, if you put them end to end in a line, about 20,000 could fit across a $2 coin.

FACT 3: They come in lots of different shapes. Some can look like balls, others like sticks and spirals. And you can use a regular classroom microscope to see them.

FACT 4: The word bacteria comes from a Greek word meaning 'small stick'.

E. coli bacteria.

FACT 5: There are LOTS of them around. In just one gram of soil there may be 1 billion. Even more amazing is this: if you collected all the bacteria living in the world's seas, the huge mass of bugs would weigh more than all the fish in the sea put together. The thing is, fish are fairly big, but their population is spread out across the enormous oceans. Bacteria are minuscule but there are gazillions of 'em in just a bucket of ocean water.

FACT 6: They live everywhere: up in the atmosphere, miles down at the bottom of ocean and inside rocks deep below the Earth's surface.

FACT 7: They thrive in the sorts of places we find freezing cold or boiling hot. Some super-cool bacteria live in the frozen North Pole, where the temperature can plummet to minus 80 °C. And others are *so hot right now* that they love to live near scorching volcanic vents on the ocean floor.

FACT 8: Some bacteria can move very fast because they have a special tail, called a flagellum, that works a little like a propeller. This bug outboard motor is very powerful; some speedy specimens can move a distance equal to 100 of their body lengths every second. Okay, they are very small, so 100 bug body lengths isn't very far – even if you were swimming amazingly slowly, you'd still thrash them in a race. But think about this: if they were the size of an adult human and sped along at 100 body lengths a second, they'd demolish the world's best swimmers in a race. These turbo-boosted bugs would swim 100 metres in about half a second!

FACT 9: Most bacteria are harmless. In fact, maybe less than 1 per cent of them give us diseases. And there are LOTS of different types of them. When scientists analysed seawater from deep in the ocean, they found 20,000 different types of bacteria in just one litre. That's not 20,000 individual bugs – it's that many different *species* of them.

FACT 10: The bacteria that do cause disease can do a lot of damage though. For example, every second that ticks by, someone in the world catches the bacteria that causes a disease called tuberculosis (TB). And every 15 seconds someone dies of the disease.

A swimmer who swallows a mouthful of seawater could, in theory, gulp down 1,000 different types of bacteria in one go.

That's gold!

Scientists have found bacteria living 2.8 kilometres underground near a South African goldmine. What makes them strange is that they get their energy, not from the heat of the sun, but from radioactive uranium in the rocks. So these bugs are actually nuclear-powered! And the *really* fascinating thing is that if there are bugs living like this on Earth, who is to say that there aren't similar bacteria thriving deep under the surface of planets like Mars?

VirUS and THEM

The story of viruses is a tale of US and THEM. Viruses can't survive and reproduce on their own – they need US to do their dirty work. And when we are infected by THEM, they often make US ill. So viruses need US, but we can certainly do without THEM.

RADIOACTIVE.

11

Viruses are small, so small they make teeny bacteria seem fairly large. Some viruses even exist especially to infect bacteria. Viruses also come in lots of shapes and sizes and types, but deep down they are really fairly simple things: an outer protein coat that covers a fairly small amount of genetic material inside.

But simple doesn't mean stupid. Viruses are ruthlessly, scarily ingenious because they hijack the cells in our body. First, they attack certain types of cells and are often quite picky about the ones they go for. Then they take over the machinery inside their favourite cell and force it to make lots of virus copies, often killing the cell in the process. Next, the new viruses emerge, sometimes exploding out when the cell bursts like a balloon, and look for more cells to hijack and destroy.

Viruses are tiny. If you put an average-sized one next to a flea, the size difference would be roughly equivalent to a person standing next to a mountain twice as high as Everest!

It's very effective, because viruses cause lots of diseases, from relatively harmless ones like the common cold to very serious ones like AIDS – some can even cause cancer.

You'd have thought it would be pretty easy to tell whether something is alive or not. Take a parrot, I reckon you could tell if it was living or if it had died and become an ex-parrot. But you'd have a problem telling if a virus was alive, because even scientists can't agree on whether they are actually living things. Viruses aren't strictly alive for lots of reasons, like the fact that they aren't made of cells and can't make more of themselves without the help of other host cells. But they are also not strictly dead: they contain genetic material like normal 'living' cells and can replicate. It's all strictly very strange.

WANTED
DEAD OR ALIVE

The word virus comes from a Latin word that means poison. And they certainly can be very poisonous.

Fungi, from pizza topping to pill popping

The upside of toast at breakfast-time is the side that's spread with tasty jam or yummy Vegemite, mmmm. The downside is when, just as you are about to take your last bite, you turn it over and catch sight of a strange, fuzzy, bluey-white patch on the underside. And you suddenly realise that the peculiar flavour mixed up with the jam isn't there because your festy morning mouth hasn't had its teeth brushed yet. It's the nasty taste of mould. You're eating mouldy bread! **Good morning, Fungus Breath!**

Yes, the mould on bread that all of us have scoffed is actually a type of fungus. But not all fungi are nasty. (It's *fungi* when you are talking about lots of them, and *fungus* when there's only one.) There are some we even love to eat. For example, fungi are used to make the dough in our bread rise and to make lots of cheeses. They are even needed to make the ingredients in some soft drinks. And there's one particular fungus that's especially tasty on pizza – mushrooms. So, next time you order a pizza, why not ask for **extra fungus!?**

Morning , Fungus Breath!

But you can find fungi all around the place, not just on pizzas. They are in the air, soil and water. Wherever we go, there is always a fungus among us. And they are very important, because they are good at eating up dead things. In other words, making things rot or decompose. Fungi are the world's original recyclers, taking stuff we throw out or is dead (like banana peels or an ex-pet goldfish or garden leaves) and turning it into useful nutrients for other living things (like tomato plants or apple trees).

14

But fungi can also make us ill. They are a common cause of irritating allergies that can make our eyes water and block up our nose. And some fungi cause extremely serious illnesses, especially in people who are ill and frail already.

So fungi can be a doctor's enemy, but, interestingly, they are also a medic's friend. Did you know that some of our very important weapons against harmful bacteria are made from fungi? You may have popped one of these pills when you've been ill. It's called penicillin, a life-saving medicine developed by, Aussie, Howard Florey.

The word mould comes from an old word that means 'fuzzy'. If you want to see a fuzzy growth of mould, get an orange or an apple and leave it out for a while.

Closing the book on amazing bugs

What? You've only just opened this incredibly cool book, and now it's going on about closing it? That's WAY weird.

You'd be foolish if you closed it up now. You'd miss out on all the amazing stories about the germs, worms and other staggeringly gross lurgies that like to live inside us. Terrors like the super-freaky bug that crawls up our nose and eats our brain,

How do companies make jeans with that (supposedly) cool, faded, worn-out look? They dip them in a vat containing fungi that eat away and digest the jeans' fibres. Jeans munched on by fungi are called 'stone-washed.' I call them 'in-jean-ious'!

15

A truly humungous fungus

What's the largest living organism on the Earth? If you think it's a blue whale or an elephant or a massively tall tree, maybe you should think again. Some scientists think the world's largest living organism is actually a fungus! This mega-organism lives in a forest in the American state of Oregon, mostly underground. Amazingly, this humungous fungus covers an area bigger than 1,000 soccer pitches.

or the 10-metre-long worm that lives in our guts, or the virus that can make you feel like your neck is as long as a giraffe's, or the African eye worm, or Ebola or the greatest plague in the history of the world!

And you'd never know just how super brilliant bugs can be, like the bacteria that makes cuts glow in the dark, and others that have outwitted some of the brainiest people on the planet, like one of the most important doctors in America, for instance . . .

Infectious bugs made a VID (Very Important Doctor) look like a right nincompoop. His name was William Stewart, and in 1969 he was America's Surgeon General. At that time, people were feeling pretty excited about how clever we humans are. In 1969, men first landed on the moon, which certainly was a spectacular achievement. But perhaps not as spectacular as the discovery of medicines that fight bacteria – bugs that had killed a huge number of people throughout history.

By 1969, these antibiotics (like penicillin), had been around for a while, and lots of people thought we were finally winning the war against bacteria and other bugs. And that's when William Stewart (VID) dropped his mega-clanger, famously declaring that the time had come to 'close the book' on diseases caused by infectious bugs. It was a bold thing to say because to 'close the book' on bugs means something like, 'Stop worrying about it, because the lab rats and I have got this serious problem sorted out.'

So, have we got the virulent viruses and beastly bacteria beaten? Is the book closed? (Hopefully *this* book is still open!)

Well, the short answer is a big 'NO'. Think about this staggering fact: today, almost 40 years on from 1969, about a quarter of all the deaths in the whole world are caused by infectious bugs like bacteria, viruses and the like. The truth is that bugs may have amazing special powers

(like glowing in the dark or making you feel like a giraffe) but lots of them do lots of harm to lots of people.

But that doesn't mean you should be scared. Many of us, especially in wealthier countries like Australia, are reasonably safe, as doctors have an arsenal of good medicines to fight bugs. What you *can* be, though, is excited and amazed and fascinated. Because the more we all know about these bugs, perhaps the better we'll be at understanding them and fighting them and, of course, living with them, especially with friendly ones, like the fungi that top our pizza and those that make the pill-popping medicines that help us feel better.

So, **roll up your sleeves**, hold your nose, snap on your gloves, strap on your goggles and mask, and dive in! There are loads of gross bugs out there, and you are about to get en*gross*ed in them. (Oh, and please don't close *this* book on bugs.)

There's a Worm on My Eyeball!

African eye worm

Say hello to the mother of all gross-outs – a worm the length of your little finger that lives inside you for years and years without you even knowing it. And then, completely out of the blue, it horrifically reveals itself in an extraordinarily 'eye-catching' way. It squirms and wriggles and writhes . . . across your EYEBALL! This monster is the headmaster and the pupil is . . . the pupil of your squidgy little eye!

Imagine the scene! One moment you are happily playing with your mates, and the next you notice a weird twitch in your eye. 'Just a lash or a bit of grit,' you think. 'It'll go away soon, no worries.' But the niggle gets worse and worse, and now it's mega painful and your eyes are watering. So you get a mate to check out what's going on. And when he stares into your eye, you see the terror on his face. 'Aaaaagh!'

H-EYE, EYE AM AN AFRICAN EYE WORM, AND EYE WOULD L-EYE-KE TO GIVE YOU A FR-EYE-GHT BY TAKING A H-EYE-KE R-EYE-GT OVER YOUR EYE! EYE AM LONG AND THIN, L-EYE-KE A THREAD OR TW-EYE-NE, AND EYE ENJOY L-EYE-FE IN AFRICA.

There, snaking through the thin, transparent layer that covers the surface of your eyeball, is a WORM! Now you are totally freaked out (like, totally). **There's a worm on your eyeball** – worms belong in dirt and filth and grime, not in eyes. Certainly not in your eye! That's the last place on earth a worm should be.

And suddenly the horrific worm is gone. It's taken about 15 minutes to slither over your eyeball and take in the sights. Now it's back inside you, wriggling its way through your flesh, unseen. But you know it's there, somewhere inside you, and you'll never forget that now – neither will your poor mate, who's still barfing in the bushes! (Come to think of it, maybe a worm on your eyeball could come in handy. You'd never lose a staring competition, and you'd be able to freak anyone out at any time – friends, teachers, parents – just by eyeballing them.)

Say 'h-eye' to the African eye worm!

This horror is the African eye worm, a dreadful creature from the rainforests in Central and West Africa where it infects millions of people living there. It's long and thin and looks a little like a piece of thread (just

20

0.5 millimetres across). Male worms grow to about 3 centimetres long, but the females can be 7 centimetres – that's a lot bigger than your eye. I told you it was the *mother* of all gross-outs.

The strange thing is that most of the time when the worm is living in us, we don't even know it's there. It lives a little way under the surface of our skin, so it isn't often seen, even though it may stick around in us for as long as 10 years. Imagine – **your skin crawling with worms and you don't even know they are there!**

Sometimes, though, the worm does surface and show itself. That's when it decides to go walkabout through our eye, and 'slitherabout' through other bits of flesh, and then we sure do notice it! As well as getting up close and personal with our eyeball, the worm can also make our skin itchy and swollen, especially around joints like the wrist or knee, because there the tendons and ligaments halt the worm's progress.

A blood-guzzling ally

But the African eye worm doesn't act alone. It needs help to get inside us and make us a home for squillions of squirming worms . . .

As the worms get a 'wriggle on' inside us, they breed like crazy and lay

Avoid the deer fly, and the worm, by using insect repellent and wearing long-sleeved shirts and long pants. If you are unlucky enough to get infected with the eye worm, there are medicines to treat it.

loads of little worm eggs. These eggs spend their nights in our lungs, but during the day they come out especially to laze around in our bloodstream and wait for a special type of fly – a deer fly with a very nasty, painful bite – to suck our blood. **And that's ingenious**, because the time when the eggs travel into our blood is *exactly* the time of day when the deer flies like to buzz down from high in the rainforest canopy in a vicious air raid to bite unsuspecting victims and guzzle their blood.

So, when the fly sucks, it's also likely to suck up a baby worm or two. Then these baby worms hatch and bore through the fly's guts into its muscles, where they do a bit of growing and developing, before they make a bee-line for the fly's mouth. And there they wait for the hungry deer fly to bite another victim, and they bite hard – these flies can even nip you through your clothes! The deer fly basically carries the worms to the next victim.

For the African eye worm, it's a remarkable squirming journey from a nasty fly bite to a ghastly eye fright.

I Pick Your Nose! I Eat Your Brain!

Naegleria fowleri

Nay-glee-air-ee-uh fow-ler-ee

Ever eaten brains? Perhaps you've lunched on braised brains in a fine port wine sauce? Or brunched on broiled brains drizzled in white truffle oil? Or maybe you've munched on battered brains with boiled butter beans? Or maybe you haven't, because just the thought of gobbling an animal's grey matter is enough to make you spew your brekkie up.

Believe it or not, some people do like to eat animals' brains for supper

– gross! But if you think an animal brain supper is super gross, how horrible would it be to feast on festy human brains? I happen to know a strange little Aussie bug that does just this. **It's a creepy killer that loves the taste of kids' brains**, served up warm and raw with a rich gravy of gooey red blood. Yes, this beast has your brain on its lunch menu, which certainly is food for thought!

And the way to its brainy buffet is a crawl through the bogeys and snot in our nose. Then it's just a short trip to our brain aka LUNCH – gobble, gobble, slurp, slurp – and we're dead quick smart, before anyone nose (sorry, *knows*) what on earth is wrong. This truly is the Bogey Man of Bugs, the Snot Mess Monster of the microbial underworld.

If you were to crack open the skull of a person infected with this brain-devouring monster and slice their brain in half, it wouldn't be a pretty sight. Their brain may be an ugly mess of **swollen flesh** that's pocked with **strange dead bits.** (Caution: this 'cracking' procedure is not advisable while the brain in question is still in use, especially if it is daydreaming, scheming and thinking up jokes.) But you wouldn't actually see the bugs that skolled the contents of the poor person's skull – these micro-munchers are only about 0.02 millimetres across!

Spooky spewy rewind

Strangely, just a few days before, this person had been quite well. Just a week ago he'd been having a laugh with his mates at a freshwater lake close to where they live. Let's call this doomed guy 'Ben' . . .

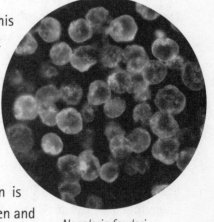

Naegleria fowleri.

The beginning of Ben's end

It's a blazing hot February day and Ben is playing with his friends in the lake. But Ben and friends are not the only ones wallowing in the warm water, because, unknown to the kids, a killer bug is also splashing about in the drink.

Its name is *Naegleria fowleri*, and it's a type of bug called an amoeba. It's made of just one cell, and it looks a bit like a sandwich bag full of fluid, with a cell wall on the outside keeping all the churning goo in. And if you search for it in the soil and freshwater where it likes to live, you'll find there can actually be quite a lot of it about.

But despite it being common, only about 200 people in the whole world are known to have had their brains picked by this bug. But unfortunately, **this little amoeba killed almost every one of the 200 people it infected**, which makes it lethal with a capital L! And the illness was first discovered in Australia in 1965 – since it's particularly partial to warm water, it loves a long, hot Aussie summer. And for Ben and his mates, it's been a scorching summer, and now the amoeba in the swimming hole is hungry – hungry for brains.

Ben is about your age – most people who get ill with this amoeba are children or teenagers – and he'll be dead in a week, but he doesn't know it. Right now he's leaping from the bank and dive bombing his mates in the water. And, as Ben plunges into the lake, a big splash of water carrying the *Naegleria* amoeba shoots up into his nose.

The end of Ben's beginning

That's how the amoeba invades most people it kills – riding along in water that gets up the victim's nose. It makes sense if you're a tiny, brain-eating bug to find an entrance into the body that's close to the food. Your snoz is its front door!

So, along with the gunk and snot in Ben's nose, there is now also a killer that's slowly making its way up to his delicious, warm brain. It crawls along the nerve fibres in Ben's nose by sticking a protrusion out from its wall, a little like an arm, and then literally pouring itself from the main part of its body into the protrusion. Imagine if you moved by holding out your arm, then **pouring your guts** into the limb, which grew really big and heavy as it filled up, until it was so massive you toppled forward onto it. And then you slowly extended out another arm, filled it up and topped forward again. That's how this amoeba gets about – it may not be speedy, but it's deadly effective.

The end of Ben

The amoeba has now found its way into Ben's juicy brain. His brain box is now a hungry amoeba's lunch box. And then Ben's end begins, because just a day or two after his swim, strange things happen . . .

First, things seem to smell different from what they usually do, and even taste weird – perhaps peanut butter tastes fishy. Then Ben suddenly gets a temperature and a bad headache, and he spews up his peanut butter sandwiches. And as the amoeba munches more of his brain, he becomes confused and can't walk. He starts to have fits and see things that aren't really there – a marshmallow in the shape of a trumpet, a shark in a top hat, a leprechaun, maybe. Or perhaps he sees his mum and dad in his bedroom, even though they are out at the shops. And in just a few days after getting ill, **Ben bites the bullet.**

The English city of Bath is famous for its ancient Roman baths. How do you think it got its name? But since the 1970s, tourists haven't been able to take a dip in the baths after someone caught the *Naegleria fowleri* amoeba and died.

One reason why the amoeba kills people like Ben so quickly is that, unlike many bugs, it doesn't need another living animal to make its home in. It can get by all on its own in the outside world in the sediment at the bottom of lakes and rivers. That's a big thing for this tiny bug, because, if its host animal dies, the amoeba can live to fight another day. It doesn't have to worry about pesky inconveniences like actually keeping something alive. Obviously, if you can only live in another living animal, killing that animal could be suicide!

Global warming on the nose

If global warming continues, the deadly *Naegleria fowleri* amoeba could have a field day, Italian scientists have warmed (sorry, *warned*). If the production of greenhouse gasses from things like cars and power stations continues unchecked, the warmer weather that would follow would be great for the heat-loving amoeba. More people would likely get infected. So, if greenhouse gases don't get up people's noses and they just ignore the problem, maybe a deadly amoeba or two will get up their nose instead.

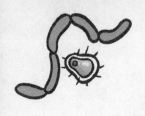

Your Su-poo-star Fart Machine

E. coli *(Escherichia coli)*

HOW YOU PRONOUNCE IT:

Esh-er-rich-ee-uh cole-eye

Many of the bugs that call our guts home don't usually do us much harm, and one of the best-known is called *E. coli.* It may only be a small, rod-shaped bacteria, but *E. coli* is a very big star in the pooey constellation – it's the North Star in the faecal firmament!

> IT WASN'T ME. IT WAS E. COLI!

For one, this tiny bacteria that weighs only 0.000000000001 of a gram is quite useful to us because it helps digest food in our gut, which is a good thing. But as it's diligently doing its digesting thing, it helps makes the stinky gas that polite people call 'flatulence'. But 'polite' isn't in this book's vocabulary, so we'll just call it by its proper name: FARTS aka trouser coughs, air biscuits, backdoor trumpets and blanket bombs. Farts are a mixture of gases made in our guts, and their active ingredients are mostly carbon dioxide, hydrogen, methane, nitrogen and sulphur dioxide. It's the sulphur gases, and a few other choice ingredients, that give them their pong.

But, despite the fact that *E. coli* is a **foul fart-maker**, this hasn't held it back – quite the opposite, in fact. *E. coli* is actually one of the most extensively studied of all living things on the planet. For example, scientists who check whether water is pure or not, so we know it's safe to drink, look for *E. coli* to see if it's contaminated with poo. (You wouldn't want to **skol a pooey drink**, would you?) The bug is also used in genetic engineering to make some really useful medicines, such as insulin, which some people with diabetes use to regulate their blood sugar levels.

Breaking wind, but not the law

In ancient Rome, Emperor Claudius passed a law allowing people to fart at banquets, because he was worried people could poison themselves if they held in their bottom burps out of politeness.

One reason why *E. coli* is so useful for study is that many strains are relatively harmless. But other strains have a dark side. If the *E. coli* bugs living happily in our intestines make a break for it and invade another part of the body where they are not meant to be, they can cause

High-tech or half-baked?

Indian scientists have come up with a strange way of stopping beans from making us fart. They found that zapping the beans with radioactive rays (before we eat them) can reduce the number of 'trouser coughs' we do.

problems, like kidney infections. There are also some types of *E. coli* that are particularly heinous because they make dangerous toxins.

One of these nasty types, called *E. coli* O111:H, caused a serious outbreak of disease in South Australia in 1995, where children ended up very ill in hospital. The outbreak was traced to a batch of a food called *mettwurst*, a sort of sausage made from raw meat.

And that's bugs for you: you can't live with 'em, and you can't live without 'em!

The art (and science) of the fart

- The average person makes 0.4 to 2.4 litres of fart gas a day.
- On average, women fart seven times a day, while men out-fart the ladies with an average of 12 a day. (This is probably because men eat more.)
- One man is known to have farted 141 times in a day. Surely he deserves a mention in the *Fartness Book of World Records*.
- You are what you eat, and you also fart what you eat, because how much you fart depends on what you eat. High-fibre foods, like beans, corn, cauliflower, cabbage and beer, are high-fart foods.
- The more gas in the fart, generally, the louder the *phaaaaaarp*! When it comes to the actual pitch of the pong, narrow bums are good for making farts with higher notes.
- In the nineteeth century, Frenchman Joseph Pujol, otherwise known as The Fartomaniac, was famous for performing farting music. When he let rip his farts, the talented 'Mr Let-Ripley' could make bird sounds and musical melodies.
- Our trouser trumpets may be contributing to global warming, because the carbon dioxide and methane in them are greenhouse gases. But animals like cattle and sheep are much bigger methane makers. For every tonne of meat produced, a tonne of farty animal methane is added to the atmosphere.

American scientist Charles Gerba is so fond of *E. coli*, he called his son Escherichia, which is what the 'E' in *E. coli* stands for.

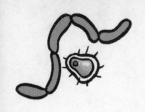

4

In the Heart of Darkness, an Assassin Strikes

Chagas' disease *(Trypanosoma cruzi)*

<small>HOW YOU PRONOUNCE IT:</small>

Try-pan-o-so-ma crew-zee

The notorious Brazilian assassin, Barbeiro, attacks his victims late at night while they sleep. And he kills in a monstrously deranged way. Barbeiro, which means 'the barber' in Portuguese, stabs his victims in the face. Then he sucks their blood and flesh through a straw, before leaving his own vile calling card – **he poos on them!**

Barbeiro is responsible for the deaths of tens of thousands of people every year. But he does not act alone. He has an accomplice! And it's not his nasty bite that kills his victims; it's his poo. Or, to be precise, a tiny parasite that's in his poo.

THE ASSASSINATOR.

SKIN AND FLESH SMOOTH

SLURP

32

The kiss of death

Barbeiro is, of course, not a person – he is actually an insect called an assassin bug. These critters, which can be a centimetre or two long, have powerful legs that grab hold of their victims and a big, pointed beak to stab them with. The beak acts a bit like a drinking straw, because once it is embedded in the victim, the insect squirts a poison down it, into their prey's flesh. Then the poison turns the flesh into liquid, which the assassin bug sucks up its beak in a sort of gruesome **skin-and-flesh smoothie**.

But that's not the worst of it, because then the assassin bug spreads the parasite that's in its poo to us, either through the place where it bit us or when we touch the poo and rub our eyes, or put our fingers in our mouth. And that's a potentially fatal step, because the parasite, which is a protozoan with a whip-like tail, causes a seriously nasty illness called Chagas' disease.

Trypanosoma cruzi parasite.

Assassin bugs are also called kissing bugs because their bites are often painless and sometimes around the mouth – a bit like a kiss!

From bug attacks to heart attacks

Just how dangerous Barbeiro and his parasite accomplices are can be illustrated by the huge number of deaths they cause. About 18 million people are infected with the parasite, and it's quite likely over a million of them will die from Chagas' disease. It occurs in the Americas but is very rare in North America. People from Mexico down to southern South America are the ones who suffer. And it's the poor who come off worst, because Barbeiro likes to do his dirty work in their homes. Many of them live in houses with mud walls that often have cracks in them, and the assassin bugs love to hide in these muddy cracks during the day. Here, they wait for the night-time, when they come down from their nooks and crannies to feed on their victims' blood.

Strangely, most people who get infected with the parasite after a bite from an assassin bug don't get ill at all . . . at first. **The really bad things start to happen years later**, in 10 years' time, or maybe as long as 40! Then people come down with serious complications, like problems with swallowing or severe constipation, heart failure or cardiac arrest, which can be deadly.

So, if you happen to go to South America, avoid staying in a mud motel. But if you really have to, make sure you use bed nets and insect repellent. Oh, and sleep with one eye open – you don't want to get assassinated!

Darwin da loser

The famous scientist Charles Darwin had a mysterious illness during much of his later life. Some people suspect it was Chagas' disease and that he caught the parasite on his world trip, while he was sussing out his revolutionary theory of evolution.

The Beauty and the Beast of the Bug World

Botulinum toxin (*Clostridium botulinum*)

HOW YOU PRONOUNCE IT:
Claw-strid-ee-um bot-tew-lin-um

What's the most poisonous substance in the whole world?

A spider's bite? I think not. A scorpion's sting? Incorrect, go to the bottom of the class. A snake's venom? Wrong *again*, now put on a dunce's cap and wander around school chanting 'I am the definition of stupid' to the tune of the Belgian national anthem . . .

All those critters may be natural born killers, but you won't come across the world's most powerful poison in something scurrying across the carpet or slithering though the grass. Nah, if you are looking for a *really* lethal weapon, you have to look down . . . a microscope.

The most poisonous thing known to man comes in fact from a minuscule microbe – a rod-shaped bacteria called *Clostridium botulinum* that makes a nerve toxin so lethal, snakes and spiders seem almost friendly by comparison. Just 1 gram of the bug's toxin, called *botulinum toxin*, spread around in the air, would be enough to kill more than a million people breathing it in. Only 20 grams, about one tablespoon's worth, could, in theory, kill everyone in Australia!

But perhaps what's *more* amazing about this wicked bug is the fact that lots of doctors use it, not to kill (obviously), but to try to make people look younger and prettier! That sounds almost as mad as Superman taking a kryptonite bubble bath, but it's true. This bacteria truly is the beauty and the beast of the bug world.

The beauty

The toxin made by this bacteria paralyses our muscles, and that makes it useful for doctors who try to make people look more beautiful.

When people grow old, their skin often goes a bit wrinkly, like an apple that's been sitting around for ages. Look at your smooth face in the mirror, and then look at someone who's old (NOT your mum, she won't be impressed at all). Can you see wrinkles on their face, around their eyes? People call them 'crow's feet'. Or maybe they have 'chook neck' or 'bunny scrunch lines' at the side of their nose.

You can make it look like you've got crow's feet if you squint and tense up the muscles in your face. If you relax the muscles, the crow's feet go away. Doctors can make older people's wrinkles less noticeable in the same sort of way by injecting a tiny amount of the *botulinum* toxin, which temporarily paralyses their face muscles.

When I say they inject a *tiny* amount, I mean an extraordinarily tiny amount: much, much less than the lethal dose. If one gram could kill a million people, just one millionth of that could do for little old you. That's why some other people in the world, who are less interested in beauty and more interested in the beastly side of this bug, come into the story . . .

The beast

Because this bug is sooooooo good at killing, some armies and terrorists have become interested in using its nerve toxin in weapons. Luckily, it's not really possible to kill a million people with just 1 gram of the toxin, because you can't spread that amount evenly throughout the air. But experts *do* think that if you had an aerosol can full of it and you gave it a good spray, it could incapacitate or kill 10 per cent of all the people within 500 metres downwind.

It's also suspected that a Japanese doomsday cult tried to use aerosols full of the toxin a few times during the 1990s. But their attacks failed, perhaps because their equipment didn't work properly.

The dirt on this multi-talented microbe

While the toxin is helping wrinkly types feel less wrinkly about themselves, the bacteria that makes it is living happily in the dirt. That's its natural home, where it can live for a long time in a dormant (sleeping) state. Then, when the conditions are just right, it begins to multiply and make its noxious nerve toxin. Our fruits and vegetables are often grown in dirt, and, if it happens to contain the toxin, we can be in deep in trouble. Food poisoning is bad enough, but when it's caused by this obnoxious toxin, the results can be fatal. Let's just say, this bug can give new meaning to the phrase 'food to die for'.

Close, but no cigar

It's believed the American government once planned to use this bug's toxin to 'bump off' a foreign leader it didn't like very much. The leader happened to like smoking cigars. So the Americans bought some of his favourite smokes and covered them in *botulinum* toxin. Since the toxin doesn't have a smell or taste, he would never have known that his 'cancer sticks' were even more terribly toxic than usual. But, according to the story, the cigars were never used.

Clostridium botulinum – dying to meet you

If you ate this bug's toxin, it would go from your intestines into your blood, which would take it to your nerves. Nerves are like wires that transmit electrical signals from our brain to our muscles. When the toxin attaches to a nerve, it stops the signal, a bit like flicking a light switch off. This causes the muscles to stop working, which can cause lots of problems, like double vision, drooping eyelids and slurred speech. Doctors have treatments to combat the toxin, but without these, things can go from bad to worse. Your arms and legs may stop working properly, and then the muscles that allow you to breathe in and out can be affected. And that can really mean **'lights out'** for you.

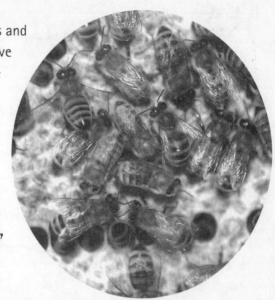

But there are simple things we can do to destroy the toxin, like heating food up before we eat it. Because most of us do cook our food, food poisoning caused by this bug – an illness doctors call botulism – is quite rare. The old saying goes that 'too many cooks spoil the broth', but they'll also spoil the most poisonous toxin in world, which is surely appetising food for thought!

Show me the honey!

Experts in America say children under 12 months old shouldn't eat honey because it can contain the *botulinum* bug's spores, and infants are particularly susceptible to infection. Strangely, honey has also been used by doctors to prevent and treat other, different sorts of bacterial infections, because it can react to make an antibacterial chemical called hydrogen peroxide. Medics have even smeared it onto sick people's flesh in hospital.

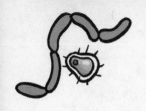

6

Warts or Hogwarts?

HPV (human papillomavirus)

How you pronounce it:

Hyoo-man pap-ah-lo-mah vi-rus

Sorry, Harry Potter. You're not real. You and your friends at Hogwarts are just made-up characters. In the real world there aren't such things as lightning bolts that shoot from wands or spells that change teachers into toads (some of them are toads already!)

But here's a truly strange thing: warts can trick us into believing in the power of magic. Yes, warts – those pesky skin growths that lots of us get – are just like illusionists who can make things like pretty women locked in boxes disappear, as if by magic.

If you want to see how, and you have a wart on your skin – or maybe a friend with one – all you have to do is try out this real magic spell for getting rid of it:

First, go outside on a night with a full moon, making sure you take mum's metal salad bowl with you. Then, carefully catch the moon's rays in the centre of it. This gives the salad bowl its special power. Next morning, fill the bowl with water and wash your hands in it, all the while chanting this powerful spell: 'I wash my hands in this thy dish, O man in the moon, do grant my wish, and come and take away THIS!' And be sure to wave your hands over the wart.

And that's it! All you have to do now is wait for the wart to go away, which it often does, though it may take a fair while. And that's magic!

But it's not really magic at all. The fact is, warts, which are caused by a type of virus called human papillomavirus, often go away all by themselves. Because they fade away as if by magic, people often think that old-school wart remedies, like the moon beam spell, actually did the trick.

That's why there are lots of wacky potions and spells for getting rid of warts. Some people think rubbing them with a coin works, others swear by strange plant concoctions. WART A LOAD OF RUBBISH! This so-called magic is flim-flam, claptrap, baloney and any other word you can think of that means 'you're out of your mind'.

So, what teaches us more about magic in the world you and I live in: warts or Hogwarts?

What are warts?

- Warts on the skin are common and are usually harmless.

- They can spread from one person to another by touching them. Picking at them can also make them spread on the skin of someone affected.

- Doctors have treatments for warts, rather than spells, but if they aren't causing problems, they are often best left alone.

- Warts frequently disappear because your body eventually learns how to fight the virus off.

Some other weird and wacky remedies

- **A very frothy botty:** A 'colonic irrigation' involves having a tube put into your bumhole (not mine!) and water pumped into your intestines to apparently flush out toxins from your guts. Sometimes coffee is even added to the mixture that goes up the bum! You could say the frothy swill that flushes back out of people's bottoms is a 'crappuccino'.

- **The bad oil on arthritis cures:** Some people with arthritis think that lubricating their painful, stiff joints with *machine oil* will do the trick!

- **Shockingly silly:** Some people strap devices to their body that send out electric shocks or magnetic pulses, which are supposed to cure cancer or deadly viruses.

CRAPPU -CCINO

Tricky Tick Tactics

The Australian paralysis tick (*Ixodes holocyclus*)

HOW YOU PRONOUNCE IT:

Icks-oh-dees hol-o-seye-klus

Australia really is a killer country. This big brown land is full of natural born killers. From savage sharks in the sea to carnivorous crocodiles in our creeks and slippery snakes that slither on dry land. And what about our little killer critters, like the feisty funnel web spider or the risky red-back? How would you like to come face to face with a gang of these nasties of nature late at night in a dark dunny?

But there's a relative of the funnel web and the red-back that's an even bigger killer than these two arachnids. And I bet you haven't even heard of it. It's called *Ixodes holocyclus*, and luckily this tongue twister of a tick also answers to a simpler name: the Australian paralysis tick. It has killed 20 people in Australia over the years, and that makes ticks more efficient killers than both the funnel web (13 known deaths) and the red-back (14 deaths).

But before you start getting frantic about this tick's killer antics, there are two reassuring things you need to know. The first thing: 20 deaths among the millions and millions of people who have lived in Australia really aren't that many. And the second thing: the last death after a tick bite was in the 1940s. That's a very long time ago, back when films were in black-and-white and long before mobile phones and home computers were invented. Today, the tick is less of a threat because doctors are a lot better at treating the illness it causes, with the help of a medicine called an antitoxin.

But this doesn't mean that we can all relax and ignore this bugger of a bug. Every year a few Aussie kids end up in hospital because they become paralysed after a tick bite; paralysed means they can't move their muscles properly. And, because this is quite rare, doctors are often stumped by the problem and don't know why the child is so ill.

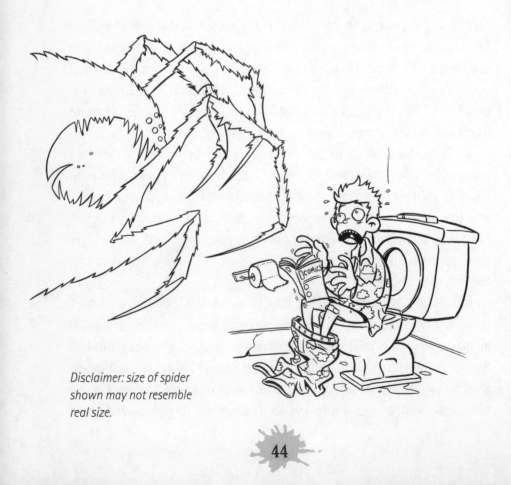

Disclaimer: size of spider shown may not resemble real size.

The tick test

Your mission is to outwit this slick tick in a test of your knowledge. Pass, and you'll escape the tick's clutches. Fail, and a fearful fate awaits. So, can you take the Tick Test? Do you have the ticker for this tricky 'tick-ey' task? Or are you too timid to try?

Answer the questions by ticking the YES or NO box. When you get an answer right, you evade the tick's trickery. If you're wrong, the tick bites you and feeds on your BLOOD. You see, this little Aussie bug needs three big feeds of blood so it can grow up from a baby into a fully grown adult. You have to stop it from growing, so don't get three wrong answers, because three wrong answers equal three meals of your warm, tasty blood. (To stop you cheating, the answers are printed upside down. You didn't think it would be *that* easy to beat the paralysis tick, did you?)

HI, MY NAME IS THE AUSTRALIAN PARALYSIS TICK, THAT'S BECAUSE I'M AUSTRALIAN, I'M A TICK, AND I SOMETIMES PARALYSE THINGS.

Question 1

Do Australian paralysis ticks live along the east coast of Australia?

YES ? ☐   NO ? ☐

If you answered YES, then you're . . . CORRECT. These nippy nasties live in a narrow band of land that follows the east coast from Victoria up to Queensland. They especially prefer wet, forested bushland. If you answered NO, the tick bit you and feasted on your precious blood. Two more wrong answers and it's a tick victory.

45

Question 2

Are adult male ticks bigger than the females?

YES ? [ ]   NO ? [ ]

If you answered YES, you are so WRONG. The girls are actually bigger than the guys. Female ticks are about 3 millimetres long, and the males are slightly smaller. Their heads have rows of tiny teeth to bite into your skin, and their bodies are shaped like little rugby balls. When they drink your blood, which they did if you answered YES, their bodies swell up to a soccer ball shape.

Question 3

Do ticks climb high up trees and jump off so they can parachute onto your head and bite you?

YES ? [ ]   NO ? [ ]

NO, 'course not, these ticks aren't skydivers; they're hitchhikers. When Australian paralysis ticks need a feed, they climb a little way up the grass or bushes and wait for an animal to brush past, and then they hitch a ride. Usually they latch on to a bandicoot or a possum, but sometimes it's an unsuspecting bushwalker.

Once on their prey, the tick does a spot of sightseeing. It can wander around their prey's body for an hour or two without being noticed, and sometimes ends up on their head, where they're often found. That's why some people mistakenly believe the ticks jump down onto our heads. So, if you answered YES, you're a goner.

Question 4

When it bites us, does the Australian paralysis tick inject us with nasty, toxic spit?

YES ? ☐   NO ? ☐

YES, when the tick bites into you, it sucks up your blood and injects its spit into your body. How nice! Tick spit is seriously fiendish stuff, because it contains chemicals called toxins that can paralyse us by attacking our nerves. The tick's toxins stop nerves from sending the right signals to our muscles, so they don't work properly - this is the paralysis that gives the tick its name.

Tick spit also contains clever chemicals that keep your blood runny. When we have a cut, our blood normally thickens, which is good because it helps stop the bleeding. However, the tick prefers to drink runny blood because it's easier to suck up. Imagine sucking a super thick smoothie up through a straw; now imagine how much easier it is drinking lemonade through the same straw.

Luckily though, most tick bites don't cause serious problems. Only an unlucky few have paralysis after being bitten, which is what happened to you if you answered NO to question 4.

RUNNY IS MORE YUMMY

Question 5

Should you tuck your clothes in to help prevent tick bites?

YES ? 　　 NO ?

YES. It helps to tuck your shirt into your trousers and then your trousers into your socks. It may not be fashionable, but I bet you'd prefer to look a little bit of a dag than have a terrible tick attached to you, which is what happened if you answered NO.

So, how did you do on the Tick Test? Did you evade the paralysis tick's perilous bites, or did you get three or more answers wrong and let the hungry tick have its feeds of blood? Now that you know the answers, why not give your parents the Tick Test and see how they do?

A true story of tick trickery

Not long ago, a small child lay in a coma in a Sydney hospital. The doctors had no idea what was causing this poor kid's mysterious illness, and they had a hard time working out what treatment would make the child better. But what saved the day was a stroke of good fortune, literally. A nurse who felt sorry for the sick child went over to the bed and began stroking the kid's head. As she ran her hand through the child's hair, she stopped on a strange small bump. There, hidden under the hair, was a tiny tick. For days it hadn't been noticed and had caused the strange sickness that had stumped the doctors. It's fair to say the tick's tricks had been foiled by a real healing hand.

Bad Luck and Bird Poo, All Over You

Parrot fever *(Chlamydophila psittaci)*

How you pronounce it:

Clam-eye-doe-fil-uh si-tach-ee

Superstitious folk would have you believe that it's very lucky to have bird poo land on you. Just like they'll claim it's unlucky to walk under ladders, that terrible things happen on Friday the 13th and breaking a mirror means 7 long years of misfortune.

But the truth is that most superstitions are about as scientific as a crocodile doing calculus, an adder adding things up or a labrador in a laboratory wearing a white coat! Which means that, at least in this book, **superstitions are super-stupid**.

Maybe proof of this is the fact that, far from being lucky, having a close encounter with bird poo can be deadly serious. Some birds' poo can be full of bacteria that cause a disease called parrot fever. This hideous affliction actually turns your skin all the colours of the rainbow, and then you start to feel peckish and develop an irresistible craving for seeds. Lastly, you go mad and say 'Pretty Polly' over and over and over again . . .

And you'd have to be bird-brained to believe that last bit of nonsense. Parrot fever doesn't mean you turn into a parrot. It's actually an illness that's a bit like the flu, with fever, headaches and general aches and pains, though very rarely it can cause super-severe complications, like a bad lung infection and even death.

But parrots and other similar types of birds, like budgies, can give us parrot fever. And what is the bacteria that causes this 'fowl' illness? Its name is – *LONG WORD ALERT* – *Chlamydophila psittaci.*

People can also come down with parrot fever when they breathe in the bacteria from dust that has come from the infected birds' dried up poo or snot. Which certainly is 'snot' very pheasant, sorry, *pleasant*! So those of us who like to get up close and personal with our feathered friends, like people who keep them as pets, or veterinarians, are at risk of getting parrot fever.

For a long time, bacteria like the ones that cause parrot fever were actually thought to be viruses because they are very small and can only reproduce when they are nestled inside the cells of the thing they are infecting.

Reassuring bit at the end

Before medications to beat this bacteria were available, about one in five people who came down with parrot fever didn't recover and died. Today there are good medicines to treat the illness, and most people don't get very ill at all. But that's the only lucky thing in this story, unlike the super-silly superstition that started it all off.

And if you have a pet bird at home, **don't stress**. There are things you should do, though, to help avoid parrot fever, like keeping the cage clean, getting sick birds treated by a vet and not kissing the bird, so the moral of the story is, never pash your parrot.

Not-so-super superstitions

Superstitions can get in the way of things, hold us back and make life very difficult. Imagine if every day your life was plagued by worries about some of these silly animal superstitions!

- If a dog howls three times, it means someone has died.
- If you give a bear a name, it will attack you.
- Never buy bees with money. If you do, they won't make much honey.
- If you hear a bird to the north, a tragedy will happen.
- If a cat sneezes once, it will rain. If it sneezes three times, the whole family will catch a cold.
- Don't cross a stream carrying a cat: it's *very* bad luck.
- An eagle sitting still means an enemy is approaching.
- Never say the word 'pig' while fishing at sea – it's *extremely* unlucky.
- To prevent bad luck after hearing an owl, you have to take your clothes off, turn them inside out and put them back on again.
- And never look into an owl's nest: it brings a lifetime of sadness.

Superstitions can mess with your life.

Not a Computer Virus, a Computer FUNGUS!

Aspergillus fumigatus

HOW YOU PRONOUNCE IT:
Ass-per-gill-us few-mah-gat-us

If your computer gets a virus, it can have hitches and glitches and completely lose the plot, while you lose your place in the computer game. Er, sorry . . . lose the *homework* you were doing. But have you ever heard of a computer getting a fungus? When that happens, things can get really worrying, because  there's more than just a game or homework at stake – lives can be on the line.

At least that's what doctors in America were worried about when they found a **fiendish fungus** had contaminated their hospital. And that set them looking for the source of their particular hospital space invader.

Now it just so happened that they made their fascinating fungus find not long after installing new computers. And when they analysed the dust inside the computers, they were surprised by what they found. **The microprocessors were full of micro-organisms!** They contained a number of different types of fungi, to be exact.

One was a bug called *Aspergillus fumigatus*, which apparently causes more infections around the world than any other mould. This feisty fungus generally doesn't make those of us who are fit and healthy get ill; it preys on very sick and run-down people – just the sort of people in the American hospital with the infected computers.

Aspergillus fumigatus.

The fungus also causes allergies and can sometimes give people extremely serious infections. Occasionally people can develop something very weird: a ball of fungus in their lungs, perhaps five centimetres across, that can even move around in the lung cavity it sits in. It can also make people cough up blood – nice!

The discovery of fungus-infected computers led the doctors in this story to conclude that the machines needed to be cleaned carefully, especially around the vent covering the cooling fan, which blows air out of the device – the very same fan that was helping to scatter the fungi around.

A worrying tale that certainly puts a new spin on the phrase 'cleaning up your hard drive'!

Holy *Aspergillus fumigatus* Batman! A long time ago in the eighteenth century, when *Aspergillus* was first being studied, scientists thought it looked like a special container that was used to sprinkle holy water around. This sprinkler was called an aspergillum, and that's how the *Aspergillus* fungus got its name.

10

Worries That Can Really Cut You Up

Delusional parasitosis

HOW YOU PRONOUNCE IT:
Del-oo-shun-al pair-uh-si-toh-sis

Imagine your home is infested with tiny mites and lice and fleas and bacteria. They're everywhere: in the carpet, on the lounge and in your bed. They're also in you, because you can feel the terrible tingle of them under your skin, crawling inside your flesh and creeping all over your body. **They itch horribly.** Sometimes you can see them, but even though you scratch and scratch and scratch at them until your skin *bleeds*, you can never get rid of these awful lurgies.

Then imagine being so desperate that you have to resort to something really drastic – **you try to cut them right out of your body**. Imagine getting a sharp steel knife and gouging a deep hole in your bleeding skin to get the terrifying invaders out. Can you imagine the horror and the agony of it all?

Now imagine how much more scary it would be if, amazingly, no one believes your story. Your family, your friends and even your doctor refuse to believe you are infested with these awful bugs. That's way scary!

But the totally creepy thing about these particular creepy crawlies is that everyone, apart from you, is absolutely right. They really don't exist. They are all in your imagination. Imagine that . . .

Nightmares and frightmares

Luckily this isn't you. You are just playing at imagining that you are imagining horrific bugs in your body. But for some unfortunate ill people, this is a real problem. Instead of being infected with bacteria or worms or lice or fleas, they are infected with just thoughts – *scary* thoughts.

But the worries that plague their mind can be just as dreadful as having a real infection, because **our mind is very powerful**. When it plays tricks on us, things that aren't really there can sometimes feel like they are very real indeed. Think how real your dreams can seem, especially nightmares, like the one where you go school in your pyjamas and then wake up totally relieved you're still in bed!

These people suffer from – *ALERT, ALERT, LONG COMPLICATED WORDS APPROACHING* – something called *DELUSIONAL PARASITOSIS*. All that gobbledy gook of a name really means is 'infection that's all in the mind', so people wrongly believe they are infested with parasites or any other bug. Simple really.

But what isn't so simple is looking after people with this problem, because it can make them suffer for ages. They can get lots and lots of doctors' examinations and tests for bugs, but all the prodding and poking and investigating and scanning reveals absolutely nothing at all. No mites, no lice, no fleas, no worms and no bacteria – diddly squat, nil, nada, zero, zilch.

And that's when people suffering this terrible torment can resort to scratching their skin until it bleeds, or cutting themselves, searching for the non-existent bugs inside. Sometimes they even send bits of their **cut off flesh** to their doctor in a desperate attempt to show that the pests that plague them really do exist.

Doctors call this the 'matchbox sign', because sufferers send their doctor a matchbox, or any little box, that is full of dust or skin or body tissue or toilet paper or dried blood – or any other gross bodily bits and pieces where they think bugs might be. And when the doctor receives this strange 'present', they may suspect that the sender's mind is playing tricks on them.

Then the doctor can help make the problem better by reassuring them and maybe giving them medicines, sorting out what's in the sufferer's mind that makes them have these super-strange worries. So, it seems that sometimes bugs that are all in the mind can bug you just as badly as bugs that are the real deal.

The bizarre world of delusions

A number of illnesses can make people have very strange delusions – beliefs that they are convinced are absolutely true, when it is really, really obvious they can't be. Here are some examples of odd delusions:

- Aliens have removed my brain!
- I'm under constant police surveillance, even though I'm a completely law-abiding citizen!
- Other people's thoughts are being beamed into my brain!
- People can *hear* my thoughts!
- People on the television or the radio are sending me, and only me, special messages!
- I'm famous! I'm James Bond! I'm a pop idol! I'm a bar of soap!

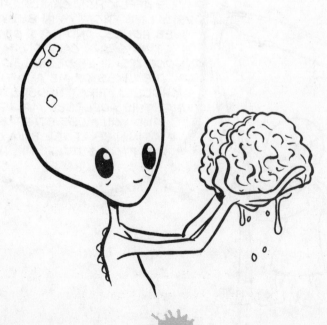

An Utterly, Gutterly Bum-blowing Illness

Cholera *(Vibrio cholerae)*

How you pronounce it:

Vib-ree-oh kol-er-ay

BEWARE THE DISEASE THEY CALL THE CHOLERA, AH, HA, HA, HAAAAAA! FOR THIS BE A HIDEOUS AILMENT THAT CAN RUSH YE TO YER GRAVE FASTER THAN ALMOST ANY OTHER SICKNESS. IT BE TRUE THAT THIS VILE AFFLICTION CAN DRAIN THE VERY LIFE FROM YE IN BUT A FEW WEE HOURS. AND SO I GIVE YE THIS GRAVE CAUTION, MY INNOCENTS: IF YE DESIRE TO AVOID THE LIKES OF ME AND THE CHOLERA, FIRST UNDERSTAND WHAT THIS ACCURSED MALADY BE. AND YOU MUST START BY IMAGININ' THAT YER BUM IS A ROOFTOP GUTTER. AH, HA, HA, HAAA!

ER, THANK YOU, MR GRIM REAPER, FOR THAT FABULOUSLY GRIM INTRODUCTION. I'LL CARRY ON THE STORY FROM HERE. YOU MAY HAVE WON FIRST PRIZE FOR GRIMNESS AT THE GRIM UNIVERSITY 'GRIMNASTICS' CHAMPIONSHIPS, BUT THERE IS ONLY SO MUCH GRIMNESS READERS CAN TAKE. I HOPE YOU DON'T THINK THAT'S 'GRIMPERTINENT' OF ME. I DO HAVE ONE QUESTION THOUGH: JUST WHAT WERE YOU GOING ON ABOUT WITH THAT WEIRD 'YOUR BUM IS A ROOFTOP GUTTER' BUSINESS?

THE GUTTER BE A WAY OF SHOWIN' YE, AND THE POOR WRETCHED SOULS WHO ARE READING THIS, THE POWER OF THIS ACCURSED DISEASE. IMAGINE IN YER MIND'S EYE A FEARSOME THUNDERSTORM, WITH THE WIND A-HOWLIN' AND THE RAIN A-POURIN' ONTO THE ROOF OF YER HOUSE. CAN YE SEE THE RAIN A-PELTIN' DOWN, SENDIN' TORRENTS OF WATER A-GUSHIN' ALONG THE GUTTERS IN A TREMENDOUS FLOOD AND A-SPOUTIN' OUT THE BOTTOM? FOR, WHEN THE LIKES OF YOU ARE AFFLICTED WITH THE CHOLERA, YE MAY BE THE VICTIM OF DIARRHOEA SO VIOLENT AND SO TORRENTIAL THAT YER BUM BECOMES LIKE THAT GUTTER IN YER IMAGININGS. THAT BE THE CHOLERA, AH, HA, HA, HAAAAAA! NOW I MUST AWAY, I HAVE SOME HIDEOUSLY GRIM REAPING TO DO.

THAT'S WAAAY GRIM, MR REAPER. I'VE LOOKED UP CHOLERA ON THE INTERNET, AND IT SEEMS YOU ARE RIGHT. IT'S BELIEVED THE WORD 'CHOLERA', PRONOUNCED KOL-ER-AH, MAY HAVE COME FROM AN OLD GREEK WORD FOR GUTTER. AND IF THE DIARRHOEA MOST OF US GET IS A DOWNPOUR, CHOLERA CAN BE LIKE A BUM-BLOWING, CATEGORY 5 HURRICANE THAT MAKES YOUR BOTTOM SEEM LIKE THE GUTTER YOU'RE GOING ON ABOUT. SO I THINK I'LL STOP IMAGINING THOSE SICK IMAGES AND START WORKING OUT HOW TO TAKE THE STING OUT OF YOUR SCYTHE AND BEAT THIS FULLY-SICK SICKNESS. LET'S BEGIN WITH THE FACTS . . .

Fascinating facts to help collar cholera

1. It's caused by a tiny bacteria called *Vibrio cholerae* that is shaped like a small comma (that's right, the punctuation mark) and has a tail that vibrates, which helps it move in water – its preferred environment.

2. In 1854, British doctor John Snow proved that cholera was spread by contaminated water, when he discovered that a water pump in London's Broad Street was the source of a local epidemic of the disease.

3. The diarrhoea cholera causes is often like water. Doctors even have a special name for it: 'rice-water stool'. 'Stool' is the word doctors use when they really mean 'poo', since 'stool' also means a small seat, like a toilet. Doctors have kooky names for other types of poo, some excellent excrement names are listed at the end of this story.

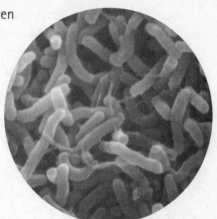

4. This 'rice-water stool' is chock full of *Vibrio cholerae* bacteria. With so much diarrhoea coming out of people's bottoms and so many bugs swimming around in it, it's

Microscopic image of Vibro cholerae bacteria.

easy to see how the bacteria can get from someone else's poo to you, especially in places where the toilet facilities aren't up to much. For example, if you don't have a proper loo and you have to poo into a river, which also happens to be upstream from where people wash or get drinking water, you can see how cholera can spread like wildfire. So most people catch cholera when they eat food or drink water that is contaminated with poo from other people with the disease.

5. When we eat stuff contaminated with the bug, it goes into our guts, where the bacteria make a powerful toxin that causes the diarrhoea. It does this by cleverly making the lining of our intestines turn itself into a sort of pump. Most of our body is actually made of water, and it makes up roughly 60 per cent of our total weight. The toxin **'pumps up the volume'** by making our guts suck water out of us, producing the watery diarrhoea that comes running out of our bottom.

6. People with cholera can lose litres and litres of fluid from their guts in just one day, and this dehydration can be seriously dangerous. If we lose so much water that our body weight decreases by more than 10 per cent, then we could be **staring death in the face** unless we get help quickly. Because people with cholera can get very dehydrated very quickly, they can be very dead in a very short time, sometimes in just hours. So that's what the Grim Reaper meant when he said the disease can 'drain the life from you'.

7. In the nineteenth century, if you wanted to wish someone bad luck, a curse was 'may cholera catch you'. But perhaps Mr Reaper was getting a bit carried away with some things, because lots of people who get infected with the *Vibrio cholerae* bacteria don't fall ill at all, or maybe only get a mild case of the squirts. But they are the lucky ones; the bug still manages to kill thousands of people every year.

8. For such a nasty disease, the way to make it better is surprisingly simple. You make sure victims don't get really dehydrated, which often means giving them special drinks to top up their fluids, sometimes along with medicines to help fight the bacteria.

Boil it, cook it, peel it . . . or forget it!

Like the Grim Reaper said at the beginning of our story: if you know all about your enemy, it's not that hard to beat him. And that's certainly true with cholera. You get it in some overseas countries from contaminated food and drink;

so be careful what you have for breakfast, lunch and tea if you go on holiday to these places. Only have drinks made with boiled water (boiling kills the cholera bugs), or buy drinks in bottles or cans. Cans of soft drink *may* be safe from cholera, but how do you know the ice that's keeping your fizzy drink cool is safe too? It's best to think twice about ice; you never know what's chilling out inside. Make sure you only eat food that is properly cooked, avoid stuff that is raw, like salads, and only eat fruit you have peeled yourself. Simple.

SPOIL SPORT.

So there, Mr Reaper. That's how to steer clear of you and the very vicious bug that can give people a severely dire rear!

The Bum Dictionary – learning to talk poo

Doctors like to talk about poo. That's because you can tell a lot about someone from their poo. Remember, you are what you eat.

There are diseases and illnesses that make you do special types of poo, like 'rice-water stool' in the case of cholera, and doctors have other special names for certain types of poo. So, if you want to talk poo, if you'd like to learn the lingo of the lavatory log, if you need to be fluent in the language of effluent, you first have to read this **Bum Dictionary**. If you don't, you'll go straight to the bottom of the class!

Bum Dictionary

Bowel movement A phrase doctors use when they'd rather not say 'poo'.

Faeces This strange word for poo comes from the Latin word for 'dregs'.

Rice-water stool The watery diarrhoea cholera bacteria can cause.

Redcurrant jelly stool An illness called – *LONG WORD ALERT* – intussusception, where one bit of the bowel folds into another bit like a telescope, can make poo look like redcurrant jelly.

Melaena Black, tar-like poo that is caused by bleeding from high up in your guts.

Meconium Thick, sticky, dark-green poo that newborn children do-do.

Pencil stool Poo that is very thin, like a ribbon. It could be caused by something blocking your guts, making only a narrow passage for the poo to go through.

Steatorrhoea Large, pale-grey, greasy poos that often smell nasty and float on the surface of the toilet water, making them hard to flush away. The poos are this consistency because they have too much fat in them. They can be caused by illnesses where you don't absorb as much fat from your food as you should.

Would You Like a Side Order of Poo with That?

Trichostrongylus

How you pronounce it:

Trick-oh-stron-guy-luhs

This story isn't about someone who piles up a plate with food, climbs up on the table, does a huge slimy poo all over their plate and scoffs the whole steaming lot in a **super pooey, chop suey feeding frenzy!** It's *not* about that. It's about something similar . . . and maybe even *more* gross.

The situation we're looking at involves people who get a dollop of ANIMAL poo, smear it all over their supper and then proceed to chow down. Now, feasting on animal droppings sounds monstrously mad with a capital M.

But, get this, there are people living among us – maybe you included – who do this ALL THE TIME. That's right, normal-looking Aussies who do dine on animal do-do, people who sometimes 'chew the poo'. And no one knows they're a member of Team Turd until a small worm exposes their strange eating habits by making them ill.

Recipe for tummy trouble.

A gut full of goat worms

The tiny worm in this bizarre scenario goes by the name of *Trichostrongylus*, and it's actually quite common in animals that enjoy eating plants, like sheep and goats. It lives in the animal's guts and comes out in their poo, and that means we can get infected with the worm if we eat the poo of an infected goat.

Now, I know what you're thinking – no one in their right mind would eat poo, a goat's or otherwise. But the reason we know that some folk do is that, every now and again, doctors diagnose people with a *Trichostrongylus* worm infection. Not long ago, two Aussies got the bad tummy illness that the worm can cause, which included tummy pain and diarrhoea. And both times their doctors suspected they'd caught the worm because they'd eaten goat poo.

The truth is that these two worm-infested unfortunates didn't actually put the goat poo directly on their dinner plates, like some sort of garish garnish or crazy gravy. What they had done was spread goat manure as fertiliser on their gardens, to help their vegies grow. That isn't so gross – lots of people do that. But what set these two apart was that they neglected to wash the goat manure *off* their vegies before eating them, so their greens came with **ready-made toppings of goat droppings!** And that's what got them stuck – yuck!

That's one big reason why it's best to wash your vegies thoroughly, especially if you don't know where they've been, or what's 'been' on them. But you knew that already, because, let's face it, not cleaning manure off a crisp lettuce leaf isn't *that* far removed from simply pouring poo-flavoured sauce on your supper. And that thought is guaranteed to leave a bad taste in your mouth!

Can't stand greens? Blame your genes!

Researchers in America have found that some people have special genes that make vegies like broccoli taste especially bitter. This could explain why some kids baulk at the sight of greens on their plate. So, if broccoli gives you the heebie-jeebies, you now have a perfect comeback when your mum orders you to 'eat your greens'. You were *born* to hate 'em!

How Medics Can Really Bug You

Here's some shocking news: doctors' mobile phones are bugged. But they aren't bugged by spies or undercover detectives who are listening in on their conversations, they are 'bugged' by bugs of the bacterial kind!

It seems doctors' phones are crawling with these microbial micro-snoops, and some experts think contaminated mobiles could help mobilise bacteria around hospitals from one sick person to another.

It's not hard to see how the phones get 'bugged'. Doctors in hospitals poke and prod lots of poorly people, who can cough and sneeze and wheeze all over them. So other people's microbes can easily end up on medics. After all, you already know that **we're absolutely covered in bacteria** – if a normal healthy person has about 500,000 bacteria on every square centimetre of armpit skin, think how many there must be on their whole body.

And that's *well* people; sick people in hospital can be a happy home to gazillions of germs on their skin, in their poo and other nasty gunk, like spit. Ill people can have vast numbers of bacteria living in just one millilitre of their spit. (If you want to know how much a millilitre actually is, you could spend a week or so spitting into an empty one-litre soft drink bottle until it is filled to the brim. One millilitre would be one thousandth of the total amount of spit in the bottle! But that would be super mega gross – imagine if someone took a swig – so DON'T DO THAT.

Because bugs are all around us, especially in hospitals, researchers in Britain tested doctors' mobile phones for bacteria. They found that most were infected, and some were home to dangerous types of bacteria that, at least in theory, could even kill a sick person, the very patients the doctors were caring for.

Handing out diseases

But contaminated mobile phones are not a very likely way for doctors to spread bugs from one patient to the next. Doctors' hands are much more handy for spreading bacteria around. When a medic examines you, some of your bugs end up hitching a ride on their hands. Then, when the doctor examines the next sick person, some of the bugs come off their hands and settle on this poor patient. A simple way to help stop this happening is for doctors to clean their hands after each time they touch someone who is sick, which lots of them do, although some aren't as careful as they should be.

The scale of the bug problem

One reason why it's very hard for doctors to avoid picking up patients' bugs is that ill people shed their dirty, bug-infested skin over them all day long. No, they don't shed their skin whole, like a snake or a tarantula – that would be very weird. Tiny flakes of skin drop off all of us, all the time. About a million skin flakes containing infectious micro-organisms drop off our body every day. Then the flakes waft through the air like talcum powder and settle on the floor and tables and, of course, other people.

That's partly why about one in every ten people who goes in for a hospital stay actually catches an infection while they are there. And while doctors try really hard to stop these unwanted infections, maybe one-third of all of them could be prevented by simple things like more frequent hand washing. And you thought people only went into hospital to get better!

Say hello to Dr Bug!

Here are some other ways doctors and nurses can be home to bugs, though most of them probably aren't too much of a danger, at least compared with contaminated hands:

COUGHS AND COLDS

Many young doctors don't take a sickie when they get crook, because they are sooo fearless (or are they scared of their cross boss?) And when these crook docs sneeze all over you, guess who catches their cold . . . *you* do, which is fully sick, NOT.

TIES

If you have ever worn a necktie and eaten soup at the same time, you'll know how easy it is to get it filthy. Doctors sometimes have to deal with poo and all sorts of other human goo, so imagine how festy their ties could get! So it's no wonder that doctors in America found that about half of the medics' ties they tested had disease-causing bacteria on them.

Getting to the bottom of the story

Sometimes doctors have to feel up inside a patient's bum with their finger – it's an important, but not exactly pleasant, part of some medical examinations. There is a story that, during one such procedure, a doctor forgot that his tie was dangling down and, not looking, shoved the tie up the poor person's bum along with his finger!

STETHOSCOPES

Researchers in Canberra tested lots of stethoscopes used in a hospital and found a few had dangerous bugs on them. They said doctors should clean up their act by cleaning up their stethoscopes.

WHITE COATS

Doctors in hospitals often wear a white coat, and it turns out that when they do, they wear their bugs on their sleeve, literally.

ARTIFICIAL FINGERNAILS

Fake nails may be fashionable, but when doctors or nurses wear them, the real fashion victim could be you. Bugs seem to prefer fake fingernails to real ones, because they like to live in the space between the artificial nail and the real one it's stuck to. Fake nails also make it harder to wash your hands properly.

Toys

Doctors sometimes have toys around their office for kids to play with. But Kiwi researchers found that the soft toys are often chokka with bacteria. That's one way for doctors to lose their patients.

Patient notes

When researchers in Saudi Arabia tested patients' files and notes, they found many had bacteria living on them. That's certainly something for greedy germs to take note of.

Personal digital assistants (PDAs)

Like doctors' phones, bugs are often found on these clever gadgets.

Medics' mask-ers of disguise

When doctors perform operations on sick patients they wear special masks that cover their faces. But do you know why they wear masks? Do they want to keep the person they are cutting up from recognising their face? **Are they secretly laughing at you?** What have they got to hide?

Or is it to help stop any bugs in their sniffles and coughs from wafting through the air and infecting the person they are cutting up?

Of course that's the right answer. When medics pick up a sharp knife and cut into people's skin and flesh during operations, it's important that they try to stop the bugs they breathe out of their nose and mouth from getting into their patient's open wound. But, if recent research is anything to go by, masks aren't so good at protecting patients from medics' microbes.

TRUST ME, I'M A DOCTOR.

Researchers in America tested doctors' noses to see what bacteria lived inside them. (Just so you know, *lots* of bugs live up our nostrils without doing us much harm.) Then the researchers waited while the same doctors performed an operation – wearing their masks, of course. When they tested the air around where the patients' skin was cut into – surprise, surprise – the researchers found that the bacteria in the masked medics' noses had spread to the air around the patients' wounds.

Perhaps the masks are really for disguise after all!

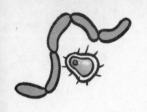

The Holy Bible, the Superbug and the Very Unholy Row

MRSA bacteria

Some books are so dull they can almost bore you to death. And some books are so heavy that if they fell on your head, they'd give you an egg-sized lump. Others can give you nasty paper cuts between your fingers (ouch!) But while a paper cut can hurt, it isn't exactly a reason to call an ambulance and get admitted to intensive care, is it? **Books are actually good for us.** They can fill us with all sorts of amazing, cool, strange, scary, bizarre and extraordinarily useful facts, just like this brilliant book does.

So it would be odd to suggest that a few leaves of paper with words on them could make you ill or even kill you, wouldn't it? But that is exactly what some scientists in England recently did suggest. They were worried that a very big religious book called the Bible – you may have heard of it – could spread a super-dangerous bacteria called MRSA through their hospital.

The Bible – Good Book or bug book?

It just so happens that in the scientists' hospital, each patient has a bedside cupboard, and in the drawer is a copy of the Bible. So, while they are ill in bed they read the Bible (if they want to), and when they get better (hopefully), the bed is made, ready for someone else to lie in, and the Bible returned to the drawer.

Of course, the next patient gets nice clean sheets and blankets and pillows - you wouldn't want to lay around in some stranger's grime and germs, would you? But what *isn't* cleaned is the Bible, and the English experts were worried that the super-nasty MRSA bacteria could hitch a lift on the Bibles and spread disease from one ill patient to another.

To see how, you have to imagine yourself in a really sticky situation. Imagine you have just scoffed some peanut butter straight out of the jar, just using your fingers, so now you have gooey, sticky peanut butter all over your hands. Next, imagine you decide to read a book, but you can't be bothered to wash your hands first. So guess what's going to obviously happen a) you're going to smear peanut butter all over the book, and b) your mum and dad are going to be cross.

Now, if your mum picks up the peanut-buttery book, she'll probably get nutty brown goo on her hands and might even smear dad with a bit. So what has happened is that the book has spread the peanut butter from your hands to your mum's hands. You have infected her with your peanut butter!

[Disclaimer: author accepts no responsibility for any parental anger resulting from experiments with peanut butter and books, especially Bibles. As the phrase goes: cleanliness is next to Godliness.]

And that's roughly how the English experts thought the MRSA bacteria might spread from one hospital patient to the next. The first patient in the bed might have MRSA on their hands and, if they read the Bible without first washing their hands, they might leave bugs on the book for the next unsuspecting patient to pick up. Remember, the bugs are tiny, so they wouldn't be seen on the book.

So that's the Bible part of the story sorted, what about the MRSA germ?

MRSA: superbug and super worry

MRSA is a big problem, especially for sick people in hospitals. It's such a big problem that it's sometimes called a SUPERBUG, because MRSA is a type of bacteria that has learned how to outsmart some of the weapons doctors use against them.

We fight bacteria with clever drugs called antibiotics, which cost millions and millions of dollars to discover and develop. You'd think bacteria wouldn't stand a chance; after all, **they're just tiny, brainless germs**. But while a MRSA bacteria will never play a game of chess or win the Nobel Prize for Medicine, it is good at one particular thing: outwitting antibiotics. So, while doctors are discovering new weapons of mass MRSA destruction, this ingenious little bug is developing ways to block our weapons.

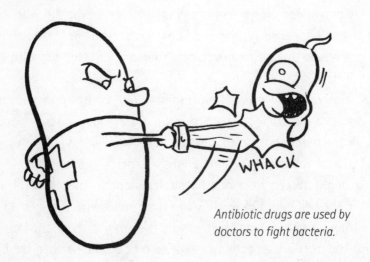

Antibiotic drugs are used by doctors to fight bacteria.

This means MRSA is harder than usual for doctors to treat – it's constantly wising up to our game. And if people who are very ill in hospital get infected with MRSA, this big bad bacteria can cause a serious infection. Because of this, doctors try to stop MRSA spreading around. Hence, the worry about the Bibles.

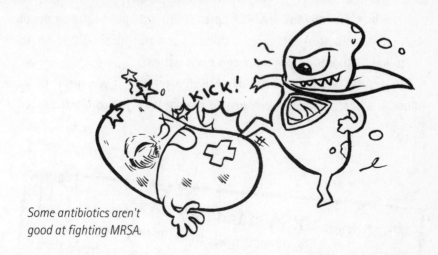

Some antibiotics aren't good at fighting MRSA.

Bad bugs and Bible bashing

There are some things that adults are especially good at arguing over. And religion is high on the list. So, it's understandable that when the English experts said they were worried about Bibles spreading MRSA, some people got very hot under the collar about all this Bible bashing. It's fair to say all hell broke loose about the holy book.

The story made headlines around the world. The idea that Bibles were risky was 'OUTRAGEOUS', some people screamed.

But once the dust settled on the controversy, some experts seemed to agree on some things:

1. Perhaps MRSA can theoretically spread from one person to another by hitching a ride on a Bible.
2. This sort of situation is very unlikely, so Bibles probably aren't much of a threat to people in hospital after all.

3. The *real* danger is doctors' and nurses' dirty hands rather than Bibles. The main way MRSA spreads around hospitals is on peoples' hands. To stop the spread, doctors and nurses should wash their hands thoroughly in between each patient.

So, peanut butter is a little like MRSA after all – if you get it on your hands, it's best to wash them, or you may get stuck into big trouble.

What does MRSA stand for?

An acronym is a word that is made from the first letter of each word in a longer name. NRL is an acronym, made from the first letters of National Rugby League. Acronyms are useful because they allow you to say long, tongue-twisting titles in a short, snappy, simple way. MRSA is an acronym for a mega tongue twister of a title: Methicillin Resistant *Staphylococcus aureus*. 'Methicillin' is a drug to fight bacteria. 'Resistant' because this bacteria can defend itself against the drug. And '*Staphylococcus aureus*' because this is the name of the type of bacteria MRSA is.

A Lousey Challenge That'll Leave You Scratching Your Head

Head lice (*Pediculus humanus capitis*)

<small>HOW YOU PRONOUNCE IT:</small>
Ped-ick-cue-lus hew-man-us cap-eye-tiss

Here's a challenge: bet you can't get to the end of this story without scratching your head. Because maybe, just maybe, your hair is crawling with tiny blood-sucking insects, vile little monsters that invade your scalp, laying minature eggs, and then spitting and pooing everywhere. And all the while they are creeping and crawling through your locks, itchy and irritating. Makes it impossible not to **scratch**, huh?

Welcome to the world of head lice. **Can you feel them now, frolicking in your follicles?** Or perhaps, when you get that itch and the irresistible urge to scratch, it's just your brain playing tricks on you . . .

> ## Sugar and spice and all things lice . . .
>
> A heady question: who is more likely to get head lice, boys or girls? The answer might surprise you.

Anatomy of a Louse

Six legs help them scuttle quickly through your hair.

Feeds on your blood and spits out irritating saliva.

About the size of a sesame seed and greyish-white in colour.

Hook-like claws enable them to grip hair and swing from one strand to another, like Tarzan.

Females lay eggs – called nits – which they stick to the base of a hair near the scalp with very strong glue.

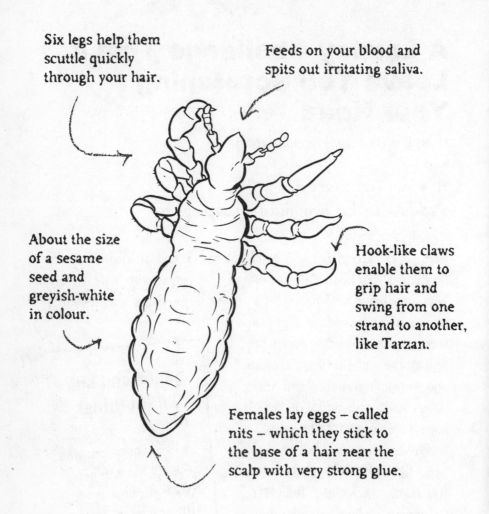

You'd probably be lying if you said you don't know about these scary scalp scavengers, because most of you have had head lice. It's certainly hard to avoid these teeny blood suckers and their horrible itch. So let's find out why . . .

A nice life for head lice

Head lice love a nice head of human hair. It's the only place in the world that they live! And they especially love your blood; it's the only thing in the world they ever eat. So it's not surprising that they have been hanging out on heads for thousands and thousands of years – they have even been found on **Egyptian mummies!**

They like our head because it's just the right temperature and humidity for them there. You could say they like the weather on our 'bio sphere'. We're great hosts; they can have a quick meal anytime, simply by biting the skin on our scalp and sucking up our blood. And, if that's not nasty enough, when they eat, they spit saliva and squeeze out strings of dark red

> MY HEAD'S ITCHING, AND SO IS MY MUMMY'S.

A bleedin' minuscule feed

Lice may drink our blood, but you'll be glad to know they aren't going to bleed us dry any time soon. Scientists from Queensland's James Cook Uni actually measured how much blood our lice swallowed during a meal and found that females gobbled a minuscule 0.0001579 millilitres and males guzzled even less, just 0.0000657 millilitres. So, unless you have thousands and thousands of lice crawling all over your head, you're not going to have to worry about losing to these suckers.

poo from their bottom, which also irritates our scalp, making the itching even worse. (Have you scratched yet?)

Lice get around by moving from one person's head to another, and they do it with the help of special claws on the ends of their legs. The claws are like hooks, which they use to swing from a hair on one person's

head to a hair on another's, like Tarzan swinging across the jungle from one vine to the next.

So you are most likely to get head lice by rubbing your head against the head of someone infested with these itchy nasties. That's why kids get them more often than adults – grown-ups don't do much head rubbing, unless they are a prop forward in a rugby league scrum, of course.

(Pssst! Have you scratched your head yet? Bet you have, you just can't stop yourself . . .)

Head lice – hits, nits and myths

Right now you're probably feeling good because your hair is pretty clean, and people like you don't get head lice, right? WRONG. It's a myth that only filthy people get lice. In fact, lice don't really care about how clean your hair is – well-kept locks are just as susceptible as grubby hair. What better proof can there be than the fact that girls are more likely to get lice than boys. Lousey girls!

And there are lots of other myths about head lice:

- **Lice crawl around classrooms searching for kids to fly onto and infest.**

That's a flight of fancy! Lice can't jump or fly – they don't have wings. And they quickly die when they fall off a nice head of hair, because then they can't get the food they love: our gooey blood.

Louse egg, aka nit, on a hair.

- **If you have lice, you should cut your hair to get rid of the itchy critters.**

That's a bald-headed untruth! Most lice nits are laid very close to the scalp, so cutting hair probably won't get rid of them.

- **Lice carry nasty diseases.**

If you've been told that, you've been ill advised. Lice may be a nuisance, but they don't give you illnesses.

Turning up the heat on head lice

Researchers believe that blasting lice with hot air from a device a bit like a hair dryer may be a good way of getting rid of them. Hot air evaporates nits and dries out the adults' bodies.

16

Finding Nemo? Finding Gastro!

Salmonella paratyphi B

HOW YOU PRONOUNCE IT:
Sal-mon-el-luh pa-rah-tie-fee Bee

Jaws or Nemo – which fish is most likely to harm YOU?

Is it the man-eating, savage shark in the horror flick *Jaws*? Or is it that sweet little clown fish that stars in the fun film *Finding Nemo*?

Okay, it's a dumb question. It's a question that puts the 'you' into ST-YOU-PID. Because, of course, one of these fish is a real threat to lots of Aussie kids. And, *of course*, the other is a great film star, but, like most stars, it isn't

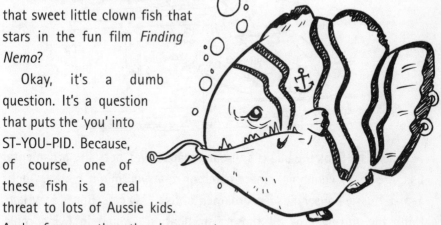

Jaws or Nemo?

someone you're that likely to actually bump into anytime soon.

Which means the feisty fish threat is . . . Nemo!

89

It seems that Nemo and his friends – the cute, colourful fish that swim around ornamental tanks in peoples' homes – have a dark side.

The age of aquariums

Aussie scientists have found that these good-looking pets may carry a nasty bacteria called *Salmonella paratyphi B*, and this bug causes severe gastro, especially in kids. (Gastro – short for gastroenteritis – is a problem with our guts, and it can cause diarrhoea, fever, tummy cramps and make you spew up your lunch.)

Scientists think the bug is a threat because 'wet' pets, like ornamental fish, are really common – more common that you might realise. About 1-in-8 Aussie households has ornamental fish. (My cats, Bones and Halo, think the prospect of all those fish floating around in living room aquariums is aquari-yummy!) On the other hand, you're not that likely to get bitten by Jaws. Shark sightings may grab the news headlines, but very few people actually get grabbed by the jaws of Jaws.

Shark attack facts

In 2005, Australia was second in the world for shark attacks, with 10 (only 2 deaths), just ahead of South Africa with 4 attacks and no deaths. America topped the list with 38 reported attacks and 1 death. These statistics don't include attacks that happen when people deliberately try to touch sharks in fishing nets or aquariums, which is a shark lark that should be avoided.

We know there is a connection between the dangerous *Salmonella* bacteria and the fish tanks because of some clever Aussie detective work. Scientists found that some people with the bug had cleaned their aquarium just before coming down with gastro. They then managed to trace the bugs in the people back to their fish tanks.

The people probably caught the bug because they put their hands into the fishy aquarium water when they were feeding their pets or cleaning the tank, and then put their hands into their mouths. So, if you insist on petting your wet pet, perhaps you should give your paws a wash afterwards. Otherwise, you might come to aquari-harm!

Dyeing to die

Some of the brightly coloured fish in home aquariums are not what they seem. Their colours might not be real because fish sellers have been known to dye their animals by putting chemicals in the tank water or giving the fish special coloured foods or injections. Sadly, this dyeing sometimes harms – or even kills – the fish.

17

Smackdown . . . Virus Style!

Slapped-cheek syndrome (Parvovirus B19)

How you pronounce it:

Par-vo-vi-rus bee nine-teen

Punching in footy is BAD, a sin bin-able offence if ever there was one. And yet the whole point of other sports like, say, boxing is to smack your fist into some poor opponent's face. For some bizarre reason, lots of people actually enjoy hitting and getting hit. I reckon that's stupidly strange – almost as strange as being hit in the face by a VIRUS!

You may not realise it, but it's likely that big, strong YOU have copped a slap in the face from a miniscule microbe. It's called Parvovirus B19 and, while it doesn't have arms to fight with or hands to slap with, this nuggety little battler can certainly pack a punch.

Parvovirus B19 is very common in kids like you (if you're not one, please give this book back to the cool kid who owns it). When this virus hits you, it can cause a bright red rash on your cheeks, just like if you've been slapped in the face. In fact, doctors call the illness 'slapped-cheek syndrome'.

That's a much better tag for an illness than **fifth disease**, which is

another name doctors have for it. Apparently, when someone very dull was classifying illnesses that give kids a rash, it was the fifth on the list – how imaginative is that?! What if you were your parents' fifth child and the best name they could come up with for you was . . . Fifth. 'Well done, Fifth! You came in sixth in Maths. A little more study next year and you'll be fifth, Fifth – maybe even fourth!'

Parvovirus B19, which is catapulted through the air in **spit and snot and sneezes** from you to me (let's hope not), must be very good at spreading around and picking a fight, because most of us get virus slapped at some time. A recent survey in Victoria found that half of 10- to 20-year-olds had been infected.

But luckily this virus usually doesn't make us very ill. Some of us don't even realise we have it, or don't get ill at all.

It may be a slap in the face, but Parvovirus B19 will probably avoid the sin bin or, in this case, the sick bed.

Curiouser and curiouser virus names

Parvovirus B19 and fifth disease are strange tags, but not as odd as some of these other virus names:

Simian foamy virus

Zinga virus

Mayaro virus

Sindbis and Ockelbo virus

Chikungunya virus

Oropouche fever virus

O'Nyong-nyong virus

Kunjin virus

How Hot Heads (and Snot Heads) Beat Bugs

You give me fever ... and that's cool

When bugs make us ill, our bodies do some cool things to help fight off the microbial villains. Sorry, did I say COOL things? What I meant to say was HOT. Our bodies actually do something HOT to battle bugs, *really* hot.

This COOL, HOT thing that we sometimes experience when we are infected with a bug is . . . a fever. The HOT feeling is our body heating up, and it's COOL because, while you might feel completely grotty, a fever is actually part of our body's cunning defence system to smash the germ invasion.

IF YOU CAN'T STAND THE *HEAT*, GET OUT OF MY SYSTEM!

It turns out that lots of bugs like to live at a certain temperature, just like we do. And sometimes these picky, icky microbes can't survive when things, or rather we, hot up.

For example, the viruses that cause flu get fairly flustered when our temperature goes much above normal body heat; that's about 37° C. So, when we get the flu, we defend ourselves by getting a fever, raising our temperature by degree or two. And if you feel ill, at least you know the virus feels even worse.

Did you know you are a cool dude in the morning and really hot stuff in the evening? Most people's body temperature varies during the day, being a little lower in the morning and higher in the evening.

Of course all this doesn't mean you have to live with a fever. Sometimes our temperature can get too high and uncomfortable, and there are remedies and medicines that people can use to bring the heat down.

Snot wars

A fever is just one of the many ways our body tries to fight off the bugs that are bugging it. We have other clever tricks up our sleeve, and up our nose. In fact, sometimes our bug defences are even on our sleeves, **for all you grots** who wipe your snot on your shirt sleeves.

Yup, that slimy secretion called snot is also a defender against germ invaders. And if you want to know why, you first have to immerse yourself in its gooey gunkyness, or at least get to know a bit about it.

DISTURBING SNOT FACT: Your nose makes a cup or so of snot every *day*, luckily not all at once. You swallow most of it all through the day without noticing. You wouldn't want to slurp it all down at once, would you?

And it's 'snot' bad stuff. Its super-soupy, gloopy gooeyness makes it great for trapping bugs and other particles, like dust, that get up our nose. So the snot stops them in their tracks, before they go any further down our throat and into our lungs. When a bug attacks and we get infected, **our sniffly snout unleashes snot hell for the alien invaders.** We also cough and sneeze, which is another of our body's ways of clearing all the gunk out of our nose and airways. It's Snot Wars, with Bogey-Wan Kenobi against Darth Invader!

Now at least you know that your runny nose knows how to get bugs on the run!

DRIP

Mmmm, snot. Your nose makes a cup or so of snot every day.

Dishing the dirt on diseases

Some scientists think dirt can help protect us against diseases like asthma! The theory is that when we are young, our body's defences need to practise squaring up against germs, and that helps ward off allergic diseases later in life. And getting grubby, like many kids do brilliantly, is one way we come into contact with the germs that give our defences the work-out they need. Researchers in Western Australia are even giving kids 'dirt pills' to see if they can help combat asthma.

Dining Out on a Dog's Bum

Double-pored dog tapeworm (*Dipylidium caninum*)

HOW YOU PRONOUNCE IT:
Dip-ee-li-dee-um ka-nee-num

Have you heard of the old lady who swallowed a spider to catch a fly that wriggled and wiggled and tiggled inside her? What about the boy who swallowed a flea that gobbled an egg that lived in dog poo that grew into a worm that squirmed and slithed and writhed inside him. Heard of him?

Didn't think so. Which is strange, because the story about the old lady with the mad eating habits is a nursery rhyme, but the boy with the worm is real – **he could even be you!** (Unless you're a girl, of course.) The worm's name is *Dipylidium caninum* aka the double-pored dog tapeworm, and it could be in a dog near you. If you thought dogs are man's best friend, you're wrong. They're just stringing us along. They only play dead for the attention and go fetch for the tasty rewards. Sorry to disappoint you, but dogs really are *this worm's* best friend.

Getting to the bottom of a mutt's guts

This dodgy, doggy worm lives in a mutt's guts, and every now and again a bit of the worm breaks off and slips out in the pooch's poo. And these worm body parts, about the size of a grain of rice, release eggs into the dog poo. Gross! But it gets grosser . . . For the eggs to grow up inside you or me, or another dog, they have to be eaten by a young flea, called a larva. That's not such a big ask; lots of mutts have fleas. And these lower life forms must like the taste of pooey worm eggs. They're certainly bottom feeders!

And the worm eggs aren't complaining. After becoming a flea's lunch, they settle in for a ride inside the cosy critter and grow up into adult fleas. Now, for you to catch the worm, all you have do is eat an infected

BUMMER!

Dogs with this tapeworm sometimes get an itchy bum and scrape their bottom across the carpet to get rid of the itch. Kids with the worm often don't have any illness at all, though sometimes they get gut pains and the squirts. The best ways to avoid the worm are to give dogs tapeworm medicine and anti-flea treatment. And always wash your mits after playing with your mutt.

flea – not that your mum makes fried flea for tea or flea and ham soup or flea soufflé, of course. But if you play with your dog and get a flea on your hands and then put your fingers in your mouth . . . that's finger lickin' good for the young worms in the flea. What a 'wonder-flea' tasty meal that would be!

Hello, maggot bum!

So, now you're a 'fear-flea' festy parent of a worm that grows inside your guts to a half a metre long – not as long as the monster beef tapeworm (see page 132), but not bad in the weird world of worms. And that's the end of the story, almost. Because, just like the worm in the dog, the worm in you releases the same small egg-carrying bits that break off its body. These little, yellowy-white worm pieces exit through your bum, and sometimes they can be spotted wriggling around in the dark recesses 'down under'.

Apparently they look like fly maggots. A maggoty bum, now that would be a truly a–bum–inable sight!

Life After Death – What a Gas!

Gas gangrene *(Clostridium perfringens)*

HOW YOU PRONOUNCE IT:
Claw-strid-ee-um purr-frin-jens

When people die, what do you think happens to all the bugs living inside them? Do you really think all the hungry microbes curl up their tails and give up the ghost too? Or that they pack their bags and look for the nearest exit?

WOULD YOU LIKE FLIES WITH THAT?

Nah, if you thought that, you'd be DEAD wrong, because some bugs think our death is dead cool. So, when our lights go out, it's the green light for them to live it up and party on down. And, in the bug world, that means gobbling our tissues so we rot and decompose.

Yes, these bugs eat us! So, when our time is up, many of us end up as a Happy Meal on the microbial lunch menu.

'Air-raising' dead bodies

There's one bug that, when it chows down on a corpse's cold cuts, can make a particularly horrible mess. When this bug eats dead people, the result can be so nasty that it often freaks out even the hardy souls who work in funeral parlours – and these people spend their *lives* working with corpses.

This bug is called *Clostridium perfringens*, and its special power is that, **as it devours our flesh, it makes gas!** And the gas does two horrible things: it smells and it swells. As it builds up – a condition called gas gangrene – it can make bodies bloated and swollen and pong something rotten. There can even be a *whoosh* of gas when funeral directors cut open the body.

If you want to get an idea of its nastiness, you could get some raw meat, seal it in a bin bag, leave it in the sun for a week or so and then stick your head into the swollen, putrid mess. It would pong, BIG TIME. It would be the King Pong! But conducting that pongy experiment would be very *wrong* and very silly, so don't.

Eaten alive

This foul decomposing bug doesn't just go for dead people. It can also cause bad infections in people who are still alive. It's quite common in the soil. And sometimes when people have bad injuries, the wounds can become infected, especially if they have dirt in them, causing gas gangrene. Inside the wound, the bug makes strong toxins that quickly attack and break down the flesh, which causes the gangrene – which means 'dead flesh' – and while it's doing that, it makes the gas.

So what does it feel like to have bacteria eat your flesh and make gas while it's at it? Something like this: the wound can be swollen and very, very painful. The skin can be shiny and taut, like a drum. As things get worse, the skin can turn dusky and then brownish-red. Thick fluid, which has a peculiar, sweet, mousey smell, often comes out of the wound, and sometimes you can even feel the gas under the skin! The sensation feels a bit like when you rustle and pop bubble wrap. So when you press your fingers on the skin, it can feel crackly. Imagine having bubble wrap full of horrible mousey-smelling gas and goo under your skin!

The bug's powerful toxins also make people very unwell, and if they don't get treatment, they can die. In fact, about a quarter of people with gas gangrene after an injury die, because infection can spread quickly while the bacteria make ultra-nasty toxins. Luckily, it's not that common today, unlike during World War I when battlefield conditions were not very hygienic and hundreds of thousands of soldiers died from it.

ENJOY THE FEED!

Maggots got that healing feeling

You thought maggots were horrible, dirty little things that you wouldn't want writhing around you at the best of times, let alone when you are very ill. But the amazing fact is that maggots love the taste of dead flesh and have long been used to treat problems like gangrene. The Surgeon in Chief of Napoleon (the famous French emperor from the nineteenth century) found that when maggots infested a soldier's injury, they actually helped prevent infection by eating only the rotten flesh and leaving the healthy skin to heal. Today maggots are still sometimes used on people with gangrene, though more common treatments involve medicines and surgery. Sometimes the affected body part has to be amputated (cut off) to stop the spread of infection or when the limb won't heal.

THE FIGHT AGAINST SLEEPING SICKNESS PRESENTS:

THE MAIN EVENT

THE FLYWEIGHT CHAMPIONSHIP OF THE WORLD

THE STERILE ATOMIC FLY (vs) THE TSETSE FLY

THE STERILE ATOMIC FLY

Home: The International Atomic Energy Agency

Special power: Blasted with nuclear radiation, so it can't make babies

Weight: Flyweight

Rank: Beginner

THE TSETSE FLY

Home: Many countries in Africa

Special power: Carries a nasty parasite that causes an even nastier disease in us: THE DREADED SLEEPING SICKNESS

Weight: Flyweight

Rank: Veteran – helps kill tens of thousands of people a year

A Big Bug Slugfest

Sleeping sickness (*Trypanosoma brucei*)

How you pronounce it:
Tre-pan-o-so-ma brew-see-eye

Ladies and gentlemen, welcome to tonight's main event. It's a fight for the flyweight championship of the world, and the lives of thousands of people. It's between two flies. That's right . . . flies! In the red corner, representing the human race, is our untested but plucky challenger. He's a nuclear-powered knuckle duster . . . let's give it up for The Sterile Atomic Fly! And in the blue corner is the undisputed champion of the world – one of the meanest, baddest, deadliest, dreadliest blood-sucking flies on the planet. The one, the only – Tsetse Flyyyyyyyyyy!

Why fly vs fly?

If you want to know why these two flies are battling it out, we have to take a journey deep into Africa. This vast continent is where many of the world's poorest people live, and so do many of the world's nastiest bugs. And high on the list of killers is a very nasty illness: sleeping sickness.

Sleeping sickness is what it sounds like – a disease that makes you seem as if you are really sleepy, but it's a snooze you might never wake up from. People unlucky enough to catch it are condemned to a slow and horrible death unless they get proper treatment, but that can be unlikely in poor African countries.

The sickness is caused by a tiny, eel-shaped parasite called *Trypanosoma brucei* that invades our blood and then wriggles into our brain. Experts think that a staggering 100,000 people a year are infected with this terrifying bug – that's roughly enough people to fill the Melbourne Cricket Ground. And they catch this killer bug from a champion brawler: The Tsetse Flyyyy!

The tsetse fly gets its name from the sound it makes when it's flying.

Blood will be spilt!

The tsetse fly is tough – it can grow to about 1.5 centimetres long – and can certainly 'go the biff'. This flying fiend gives us a mega-painful bite when it feeds on our blood, thanks to its strong, pointy mouth parts. But the pain is the least of our worries, because the fly can carry the *Trypanosoma brucei* parasites and can leave them behind in us as it's happily sucking up our blood.

So, how do you stop people from getting sleeping sickness? You first have to stop the tsetse fly. Simple . . . NOT! Tsetse flies, like many other insects, aren't that easy to get rid of completely. Think about the last time you were plagued by persistent mozzies or blowflies. We need more than a can of bug spray and a fly swatter to beat the tsetse.

DID YOU JUST TELL ME TO BUZZ OFF?

But the pesky tsetse does have one chink in its armour: how it makes babies. The female tsetse fly usually only mates once in her short life, and after that she can continually produce baby flies. And, very strangely, she doesn't lay lots of eggs that turn into maggots, like other flies do. **Every 10 days or so, just one teeny, weeny tsetse baby grows inside her.** She then lays it in a nice shady place, where it hatches a month or two later. It would be cute if she wasn't such a brute.

So, if you can stop the fly mating properly, you can stop them having babies, which will mean no more grown-up tsetse flies to spread the parasites. Hey, presto! No more sleeping sickness. And that's where the hero in this story enters the ring. Maximum respect for our challenger . . . The Sterile Atomic Fly!

Tsetse flies are particularly attracted to the colour blue. So don't wear jeans in the jungle!

The buzz on the sterile atomic fly

The sterile atomic fly is actually a type of male tsetse fly that's been transformed in a laboratory so it can't make babies. It was developed by an organisation called the International Atomic Energy Agency, which helps put nuclear technology to good use. (Nuclear war: VERY BAD. War against sleeping sickness: VERY GOOD.)

Agency scientists took normal male tsetse flies and zapped them with a dose of nuclear radiation – not enough radiation to kill them, but enough to affect their internal organs so they can't reproduce. The zapped flies are now 'sterile': they can mate with a female, but she won't ever have babies. (Because she only mates once in her life, she's now not going to be interested in any hunky fly guys that haven't been zapped with radiation.)

Scientists have released lots and lots of sterile atomic flies into the African bush, hoping that they will get together with females and sabotage them so they won't produce any more baby flies. And, if it all goes to plan, tsetse fly numbers should go down for the count.

At least that's the theory. But, like all big fights, you never really know how it's going to turn out. We'll just have to wait and see if the sterile atomic fly can deliver the knockout punch.

Early last century, treatments for sleeping sickness contained the poison arsenic. The danger became apparent in one incident when hundreds of people became blind after having too high a dose. Today, some treatments are still based on arsenic and can be very toxic, though not so bad as before.

What's it like to have sleeping sickness?

At first, the tsetse fly bite leaves behind a painful red mark. Then you may feel off colour with a fever, headache and sore muscles. Later, when the parasite invades your brain, it can get much worse. You may become confused, slurring your words, and have problems concentrating and walking, just as if you were very, very sleepy, while at other times you might suddenly become very violent – it's said that in some African villages, people with sleeping sickness are tied up to stop them from hurting other people. Then, as the disease gets even worse, you may have to sleep all through the day, but not be able to sleep properly at night. Without treatment, the symptoms grow worse and worse until eventually you die.

The Wheel of (Mis)fortune

Rotavirus

'Diarrhoea ROCKS!'

That's my motto. I'm a bug called Rotavirus, and I give lots of kids diarrhoea. I lurrrrrve sloppin' out the stuff. I love it enough to live in it.

Who needs to lay logs, when you can squirt bucket-loads of lovely stinky liquid diarrhoea. Poo just floats around like Nigel-No-Friends – what a waste of space! Diarrhoea spurts and squirts and splashes all over the place, so it's *much* better at spreading me around.

'When you're sitting on the dunny, and you're feeling kinda funny – diarrhoea (clap, clap) diarrhoea.'

The 'rota' in rotavirus is Latin for 'wheel', which is this bug's shape. Think how other words like 'rotate' also relate to 'wheel'.

I get around partly because I'm minuscule, just 0.0000001 metres across. So there can be a bottom-bendingly vast amount of me in a tiny amount of diarrhoea. If you were crazy enough to fill a one-litre drink bottle full to the brim with the diarrhoea I cause, there could be as many as ten trillion of me in there!

From my runny poo to you

With so much of me around, I'm easily spread from one kid's diarrhoea onto another kid's hands. Then all they have to do is stick their hands in their mouth, eat me up and it's welcome to Gastro-ville.

Wipeable words for boiling bums

From skittles to squits, to squirts, to splats, to bottom spew splashes, people have lots of different nicknames for diarrhoea. Recognise any? The trots, mud butt, Bali belly, Aztec two-step, the thunder from down under, backdoor vomits, runny rump and chocolate fountain.

People say the proof of the pudding is in the eating. And here's proof that kids are very good at spreading diarrhoea around from hand to mouth: **almost everyone in the world gets infected** with me before they have reached five years old. And every year 10,000 or so Aussie kids have to go into hospital, because I make them sick and they lose too much of their body fluids in their diarrhoea. That means they can become dangerously dehydrated. In poor countries, where clean water and good medical care are scarce, hundreds of thousands of kids die every year.

'When you're climbing up a ladder, and you hear something splatter – diarrhoea (clap, clap) diarrhoea.'

Little Aussie battler

It's strange if you haven't heard of me, since I'm the little battler making so many kids suffer, but also because I'm a true-poo Aussie. I was discovered in Australia in the 1970s.

The famous scientist and former Australian of the Year Sir Gustav Nossal once called my discovery 'a great hallmark of Australian science', and it certainly opened up a way for scientists to make weapons against me. And the sad truth for me is that today there are vaccines available that kids can have to prevent me from getting my pooey hands on them.

'When it's dripping down your leg, like a warm, raw runny egg – diarrhoea (clap, clap) diarrhoea.'

BREAKING NEWS: 'An attack from the notorious Rotavirus was thwarted today when kids washed their hands properly after going to the loo. Details from the dunny later in the broadcast.'

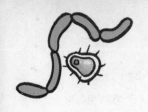

23

Jaw-droppingly, Flesh-rottingly Bad Misunderstandings

Leprosy (*Mycobacterium leprae*)

HOW YOU PRONOUNCE IT:

My-ko-back-tee-ree-um lep-reye

UNCLEAN!

This bug has a bad reputation for horribly rotting people's flesh away and then making their fingers and toes and arms and legs literally drop right off. No wonder the rod-shaped bacteria called *Mycobacterium leprae* that causes leprosy is right up there in the microbial world's **Hot 100 Horribly Horrifying Hit List.**

In fact, this bug has been top of the terror charts for thousands of years – Indian writings from as early as 600BC mention leprosy! That's given us a very long time to get very good at being very scared of it. You could even say that most of us would give an arm and a leg to avoid it!

Since the Middle Ages, people with leprosy have been treated badly by others who are scared of catching the disease. At that time, people with leprosy – called lepers – were thought of as 'unclean' and 'sinful' (bad to the bone) and were often made to wear special clothes so people would know to stay away from them. They also sometimes carried around a bell to warn people they were approaching. Occasionally they were even forbidden to touch food in the market and had to point at things they wanted with a stick.

Often, to avoid all this trouble, lepers were simply sent to a special place, far away from all the well people, where they had to live with all their fellow sick bug buddies. Later, some of these unfortunates were even shipped to islands in the ocean where it was hoped that they'd be far enough away to stop them from spreading their disease to anyone else. People were so scared of coming into physical contact with

Amazingly, a leper colony still exists today in Hawaii. From the mid 19th century until 1969, about 8,000 people were exiled to the Kalaupapa colony on the island of Molokai, and there are still a few elderly residents with the disease left there.

the disease that they made lepers use special money. So there would be absolutely no chance that the disease could spread on loose change used by well people! And so lepers lived, and died, on these isolated islands, out of harm's way, while everyone else tried hard to forget all about them.

HOWEVER, it turns out that much of what people think about leprosy is absolutely, completely, totally and utterly WRONG. Leprosy is really easy to catch off other people? WRONG! People who don't have the disease are in terrible danger if they go near someone with the bug? WRONG! The leprosy bacteria makes your arms and legs drop off? WRONG! This is a bug that has been massively misunderstood.

Look before you leper

So, sadly, sending lepers off to colonies to spend their play money and die as outcasts was just a little bit of an overreaction. We now know the leprosy bug is very sluggish and slow to grow and reproduce. **Most of us are naturally immune to its nastiness**, so we won't get the disease anyway, even if we get up close and personal with people carrying the bug.

And, if we do get ill, the leprosy bacteria doesn't rot flesh and make bits of us fall off. What *actually* happens is that the bug can attack the nerves that carry signals from our skin to our brain, telling us when we have touched something. When these nerves are damaged, we can lose feeling in our skin. And if our skin is numb, small cuts can easily go unnoticed. And these cuts and get infected by *other* bugs, and it's these bugs that can cause the serious damage.

Despite all this, lots of people do still get leprosy – hundreds of thousands every year – mostly in poor countries in South America, Africa and Asia. But now doctors have good medicines to give sufferers that can kill the bacteria.

Righting the slights and wrongs

Even though doctors discovered the truth about the disease, leprosy's nasty reputation lives on at large today. In fact, its name is so famous that it's given to anyone we like to hate or ignore. Look up 'leper' in the dictionary and you'll find it also means 'someone who is ignored or despised'.

Imagine if a disease was called 'jerky' and you got it. Suddenly, just because you had 'jerky', everyone – even your doctors – called you a 'jerk'! Wouldn't be so nice, would it, Jerk?!

Since the words 'leprosy' and 'leper' have come to stand for so many bad and unfair things, doctors are trying to make the world think better of people with leprosy and have changed its name. So today leprosy is called Hansen's disease, after the Norwegian scientist who discovered the bacteria in the 1870s.

I guess leprosy proves that sticks and stones can break your bones, but words really can hurt you.

Every Breath You Take . . .
There'll Be Poo in You!

Dust mite (*Dermatophagoides pteronyssinus*)

<small>How you pronounce it:</small>
Derm-at-toe-fa-goy-deez ter-on-iss-eye-nus

What's it like to breathe in poo? To take a big breath and suck poo deep into your lungs? Do you want to know what it feels like? Do you want to try it? No, you'd rather not?

Well, maybe you just did! That last breath you took could have had poo in it. And that one too!

DISTURBING REVELATION: Most of us live in homes that are covered in poo. Our carpets are caked in it, our beds splattered with it, and, because it's very lightweight, the poo in question can get blown up into the air we breathe. Oh dear, you just sucked some more in.

Poo who?

Just so you know, the poo in this story isn't dog poo, cat poo or even your poo. So, just who did the poo? The answer is a micro-monster just half a millimetre long called a house dust mite, a noxious nasty that lives in the dust that settles everywhere in our homes.

Luckily, the mite is too small to see with the naked eye, because if you did eyeball it as it crawled over your doona, it would probably scare the living daylights out of you. This fearsome critter is covered in a tough shell that resembles body armour. It has a mouth that looks like a pair of pincers, eight stubby legs, no eyes or wings, and hairs sprouting from its oval-shaped body.

The truly creepy thing about dust mites is that they are all over the place. A used mattress may have as many as 10 MILLION mites inside it, and they are especially common near the Australian coast because they love the warm, humid weather there. So, chances are you share your home with a mighty large number of mites – more than 1,000 can survive in just 1 gram of dust! (A gram is about the weight of a paperclip.) Now, if these facts don't creep you out, perhaps you should sleep on them, and your infested mattress!

Most of the dust particles you can see floating in a sunbeam are actually tiny flakes of human skin.

And, as we now know, these mites sure like to poo – every day one mite can drop about 20 micro poo particles. Nice! And wherever we are, there's always lots of dust around for them to live in. But that doesn't mean your house is filthy – the reason why we can't escape dust is because our *bodies* actually make it.

One of the main ingredients of dust is our skin. **Dead skin.** Small flakes of skin are falling off us all the time and settling on tables, blankets, TVs – everything – as dust. In fact, we lose about half a kilogram of skin every year in this way. No getting around it, we are dust factories, and guess what's on the menu at the dust mites' favourite dusty *pest*aurant?

Dining out on dead skin

You guessed it, Poo Breath! Our dead skin flakes are one of the dust mite's tastiest foods. So their poo that we breathe in is actually digested dead bits of us!

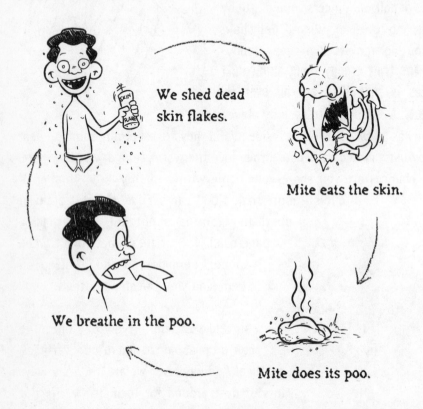

We shed dead skin flakes.

Mite eats the skin.

We breathe in the poo.

Mite does its poo.

And it gets worse. Dust mite poo also contains powerful chemicals that can make us ill. Lots of us are allergic to these toxic poo pellets, so, when we get the chemicals on us or breathe them in, they can cause problems like a runny nose, sneezing, watery eyes and skin rashes. People who are especially sensitive to the chemicals can have asthma, breathlessness and wheezing.

So, the monstrous house dust mite doesn't bite or sting or give us nasty bacteria or viruses; it harms us with chemical warfare in the form of **minuscule poo bombs!**

Mite Factoids

- Dust mites don't like bright light, so they hide away in places where we spend a lot of our time, like beds and sofas.

- Much of the dust in houses is actually made up of tiny skin scales that we continually shed. The mites eat the scales, as well as things like fungi and pollen.

- Because they don't weigh much, mites can easily get wafted up into the air when we make our beds and plump our cushions. There are always some drifting around the house.

- People who are allergic to these critters' poo can do things to help reduce dust mite numbers, like removing carpets and replacing soft toys with wooden or plastic ones. So long, Teddy!

The zoo you sleep in

Another food dust mites graze on (besides our skin scales) is fungus, and there's trough loads of that in a place you'd least expect: your bed!

Researchers in the UK found that every night we rest our head on big, soft, comfy bags full of millions of fungus spores. These bags are called pillows! Apparently, pillows are great places for fungi to live because we usually don't wash them. Fungi also like damp places, **which means our beds are fantastic**, because we sweat lots when we're asleep.

One of the researchers suggested that house dust mites and the not-so-fun fungi lived together in a sort of mini zoo. Maybe the house dust mites ate the fungi, and then the fungi lived off the mites' poo. (He also added that the research wasn't reason to chuck out our pillows.)

Does your heart fill with fear when the sun streams though the window, lighting up the air and all the thousands of tiny dust particles floating through it? If this gives you goose flesh, maybe you suffer from amathophobia. That's a fear of dust, in plain English.

So, chances are, your bed – the place where you spend a third of your whole life – is alive with micro-monsters: bugs that live off each other, love your warmth, your smelly sweat and the skin you shed. All this action happens as you slumber, blissfully unaware of the zoo that's sharing your bed with you. Sleep tight!

How Flea Spew Changed the World

Bubonic plague aka the Black Death (*Yersinia pestis*)

Yer-sin-ee-uh pest-iss

Great discoveries change history. Wars change history. Even politicians can change history. But few things have made such a massive difference to the world as . . . flea spew!

Yup, a dollop or two of slimy, blood-spattered flea chunder completely changed the world we live in. It helped change the language we speak, and it even helped change the way we work. And, if you're wondering how it accomplished these wonderful, highly chunder-ful feats, the answer lies at the bottom of a filthy flea's guts.

Dripping blood, running rats and cunning bugs

Inside this particular flea's innards, there's a lot of blood sloshing around – rat blood, actually. Not long ago, the hungry flea grabbed a bite for lunch, literally – it bit into a rat and feasted on the critter's delicious red blood.

But the little flea has a small problem, a microscopic problem to be exact. Because the rat it called lunch was infected with bacteria called *Yersinia pestis*, and now these microbes are gurgling around inside the flea's guts, along with the rat blood, doing their dirty work.

Yersinia what's-its-face – it's a long name, so I'll just call it the PLAGUE, because that's the disease it causes – is multiplying and multiplying and multiplying inside the flea. Before long, there are so many bacteria that they completely block the flea's stomach so no blood can get through it. **Not good, not good at all.** The flea starts to

starve, and when fleas get hungry, they bite more and more.

Trouble is, when they bite more rats, they can't swallow the blood properly because their guts are still blocked with plague bugs. They chomp on their rat rations and then have to spew blood and plague bugs back into the bite. So more rats get infected with the plague bugs, which kill the rats, and eventually the hungry, chundering fleas starve to death.

YOU DIRTY RAT, YOU KILLED MY *BROTHER.*

When dead rats are dead wrong

Okay, so now you're thinking, how could a bacteria that makes rats die and fleas spew completely change history? Well, it did, a long time ago in Europe in the 14th century when it's believed the plague bug, with the help of the spewing fleas, caused one of the worst outbreaks of disease ever. At the time it was called the Black Death: 'Black' because it was *seriously* grim and 'Death' because it killed a *seriously* large number of people.

Outbreaks of plague killed too many rats, and that left lots of hungry fleas, brim full of bacteria, looking for other places to have lunch. And if they can't find a rat to bite, then guess who they'll settle for? That's right . . . you. So, about 650 years ago, the Black Death plague swept through the population of Europe with devastating consequences: it killed about one in three people!

Getting plagued by the plague

You probably wouldn't even notice the place where the infected flea bit you. But a few days later, you may start to feel very unwell,

Flea.

with a fever, headache and painful, swollen lymph glands, called buboes. These give it the name bubonic plague. The plague bacteria congregate in the buboes and spread from there around the body. When the bug infects the lungs, it causes pneumonia, and you cough up bloody spit. Without treatment, many people with this disease die quite quickly. And there certainly wasn't much medical help around in the 14th century, and that's why so many millions were slayed by the plague.

The Black Death: back to the future

What would happen today if an illness tore through Australia and the rest of the world, killing one in three of us – one in three kids in your class, one in three of your teachers, one in three footy players, one in three pop stars, one in three TV presenters. In fact, it's almost impossible to imagine, because it would completely change the world.

14th century plague myth-understanding #1: After the plague started, doctors in Paris blamed it on the position of Saturn, Jupiter and Mars in the sky at 1 pm on 20 March 1345. That's an excuse that's out of this world!

In the 14th century the Black Death changed the world in ways that still affect us today. For one thing, it killed lots of rich, educated people in England who didn't speak English (unlike more 'common' people, called 'commoners'). Instead, they talked in French, which was often used for official business. The deaths of so many French-speakers went a long way in helping English become the official language of England. It also explains why you are reading it right now. Who knows, if it

14th century plague myth-understanding #2: The Pope thought the plague was caused by a foul atmosphere, so he used fire to purify the air. Poor people couldn't afford to keep fires burning, so they breathed in stale wee (urine), which they thought would make the air safer! 'Urine' trouble if you resort to desperate measures like these.

wasn't for the plague bug and flea spew, this book might have been written in French!

Because the plague bug killed so many, there was also a severe shortage of people with skills, like blacksmiths or carpenters. That meant their skills were valued much more highly. And so rich people – like kings, lords and barons – had to compete for their services by offering them better pay and working conditions. This, some people think, was the beginnings of how we do business today, with companies competing with each other for the best people to work for them and earn a lot of money. Before the Black Death, these kinds of workers were treated much more like slaves.

All this was quite a feat for the plague bug – a tiny bacteria that's spread in flea vomit!

Today, there isn't much plague around. Each year only a few thousand human cases are reported around the world, and none in Australia. So, while Australians sometimes have to worry about plagues of mozzies, or mice, or bluebottles in the sea, at least we don't have to lose sleep over plagues of plague!

BEWARE GLOBAL AND *GERBIL* WARMING
Researchers have warned that global warming could cause plague to thrive. They studied gerbils in central Asia and found that a 1° C increase in temperature in spring led to a 50 per cent increase in the number of gerbils with the plague bacteria.

26

Blood, Sweat and Fears!

Ebola *(Ebolavirus)*

How you pronounce it:

Ee-bow-luh-vi-rus

This tragedy begins in 1976, deep in the heart of Africa, in a mysterious country called Zaire. A man, we'll call him Mr X, is sick. He's got a raging fever and nurses at the local hospital think he has a disease called malaria, which is quite common in these parts. So they give him an injection for it. And then, without a second thought, they send him home to rest. It's all very routine, something that happens on most days here. But what follows is far from routine; what follows is an extraordinary disaster that will send shock waves around the world . . .

When Mr X goes home, **something strange and terrifying happens** – he starts bleeding, but not from a cut, from his mouth, eyes and nose! And very soon, Mr X is dead.

The women in Mr X's family give him a traditional funeral. As is the custom in this part of Africa, they scoop out blood and other organs from his body with their bare hands to prepare his body for the funeral ritual. And soon after, most of the women are also dead.

The Ebola virus is shaped like a long narrow filament.

But that's just the start of the deaths. Because, back at the hospital, the nurses are giving other patients injections with the same needle they used on Mr X. And now lots of these patients are also rapidly dying of the same awful disease.

Ebola is named after the Ebola River in Zaire, a country which nowadays is called the Democratic Republic of Congo.

This is Ebola, a virus that has become very famous since it emerged and caused an outbreak similar to this in Zaire. It's so feared because it's one of the most deadly diseases known and it lurks in the shadows, striking from seemingly out of nowhere and causing bizarre and unpleasant symptoms. Oh, and there is no cure for it.

Blood and guts
People with Ebola first feel weak with a fever, muscle pains, headache and a sore throat. Then they may have vomiting and diarrhoea, among other things. And in severe cases they bleed from the body's openings, like the eyes, nose, gums, ears or bottom.

Killer hospitals

Strangely, after emerging in the mid-1970s, Ebola disappeared, only to come back again 10 or so years later. And since then there have been regular outbreaks in Africa, in which a staggering 50–90 per cent of people who have fallen ill have died.

Adding to the mystery surrounding Ebola is the fact that no one knows exactly *where* it comes from. Scientists believe the virus lives naturally in the African rain forests in a certain type of animal, but they don't know which type. Some scientists suspect that bats may be the virus's natural carrier.

What they do know, though, is that when people catch this deadly virus, things quickly get deadly serious, especially in hospitals like the one Mr X went to. Hospitals can actually make Ebola outbreaks worse instead of stamping them out. The virus spreads when people get blood and other fluids (like sweat, spew or diarrhoea) from infected patients on themselves. (That's why Mr X's relatives died.) And because it makes its victims spew and have diarrhoea and bleed from strange places, like Mr X did, there are often lots of body fluids splattered around, full of the Ebola virus.

So, hospitals full of people with Ebola are dangerous places. And when outbreaks happen, often lots of people in hospital catch the bug, making the situation much worse. To stop this, Ebola patients are isolated from everyone else, and their doctors and nurses have to wear special protection, like masks and goggles. (Sometimes scientists who have to deal with Ebola can look more like astronauts in space suits than doctors.) But you can imagine how scarce these things can be in very poor hospitals where outbreaks can strike. In Mr X's hospital, when the nurses mistakenly gave him the injection against malaria, they even had to use the same needle on lots of other people. And because it wasn't cleaned properly between injections, the needle also spread the virus to other patients.

Ebola's special power is that it can turn hospitals from lifesavers into killers!

27

Super Worms, Supermodels and Super Myths

Beef tapeworm (*Taenia saginata*)

How you pronounce it:

Tay-nee-uh sag-in-at-uh

Have you heard the amazing story about the supermodel and the monster tapeworm? You haven't? Well, listen up, it's a doozy . . .

Supermodels who strut down fashion show catwalks often have to be really, really thin. Like beanpoles with long legs and painted with loads of make-up – more colourful than parrots! But the supermodel in this story was supernaughty. She'd piled on a few extra kilos – GASP, mother of all sins! Instead of being on the catwalk, this not-so-supermodel was *really* in the doghouse.

So, to make herself ultra slim again, she came up with a cunning plan: she infected herself with a tapeworm! Easy! She brought a **skanky piece of meat riddled with tapeworms** and ate it all up . . . raw. And this dirty, desperate measure did the trick. As the worm grew longer and longer inside her intestines – longer than you could imagine a worm could be – it gobbled up the food that flowed down her guts, making her super thin.

Over the years, the worm in her intestines grew to a cool 10 metres long, and the model grew very attached to her secret worm (which she named Beefy). Sadly, however, this relationship didn't have legs in the long run, because eventually the time came when the supermodel decided to hang up her designer boots. And that meant she no longer had to be quite so thin. The supermodel no longer needed the super worm.

In order to dump the tapeworm, she came up with a piece of sizzling trickery, or should I say *sausage-sizzling* trickery. She fried a snag and held it out between her lipstick-red lips. Then she waited . . . and waited . . . and waited. Eventually **the hungry tapeworm smelled the sausage lure** and slithered up her gullet, all 10 metres of its slimy tapewormyness, until its head poked out of her mouth. Beefy then bit into the bait, and she was able to pull and pull on the sausage, dragging the startled worm out of her. And when it was completely out, Beefy slithered down a nearby drain, never to be seen again.

What an AMAZING story!

And it would be even more amazing if it was all TRUE! *(Legal disclaimer: this tale is fictitious. No supermodels or tapeworms were harmed in the making of this story. Actual facts may not resemble real facts.)*

Tapeworm hits and myths

Yup, if you believed every bit of this gory story, then you've been SUCKED IN. But that's okay, lots of people think this story is true – it's what's called an urban myth.

133

More fantastical urban myths

Really falling for it: If you are in a lift that breaks and plummets to the basement, you can survive by jumping up just as the lift is going to crash.

A croc of . . . alligators: Alligators live in the New York City sewers, because they are flushed down the toilet by people who have them as pets but no longer want them.

Talkback teeth: People have been known to pick up radio signals through their tooth fillings. They are called rock 'n' molars!

But only *some* of the story is fake – bits of it are *completely* true and *completely* amazing. Your task is to separate the mythical morsels from the true testimony. And that means you have to play the *Tapeworm Hit and Myth Game*. All you have to do is read the facts from the supermodel story below and guess whether they are HITS (true) or MYTHS (false).

1. Tapeworms can grow to 10 metres long inside our intestines.

HIT ? ☐ or MYTH ? ☐

Believe it or not, this is a HIT. There is such a thing as a 10-metre-long tapeworm that lives happily inside our intestines. It's made of a smallish head, which attaches to our intestine wall, and then lots and lots of flat, rectangular sections that grow off it in a long chain. This makes the worm look like a length of tape, and there may be one or two *thousand* sections.

If you think about it, the idea of a 10-metre-long worm in us is quite weird – most adults are only about 2 metres tall, so how can such a mammoth worm fit inside us? Or do only mega-tall basketballers get tapeworms? No, any of us can get a super-long tapeworm, and the reason why is to do with the shape of our guts.

If someone were to open your tummy (it's best not to try it), you'd see that your guts don't run in a straight pipe from your stomach to your bum. If that were the case, they'd be less than a metre long. Your intestines are all coiled up and fitted snugly inside you, so you actually have metres and metres of this long 'poo tube'.

The tapeworm can grow and grow inside you to a super-long length comfortably for 30 or so years! Quite a *long* friendship!

A very long worm with a very long life span

Thirty years is a long time for a worm to live in us. Compare it with the average life spans of some other animals:

Cat	9-15 years
Dog	7-18 years
Horse	20 years

2. You can catch a tapeworm from meat.

HIT ? ☐ or MYTH ? ☐

This is also a HIT – I'd STEAK my life on it! This long worm is also called the beef tapeworm, because we get it from infected, undercooked beef. Millions of poor people around the world have it inside them, though it's not at all common in Australia because the meat we buy in shops is carefully processed, checked and cooked before we scoff it.

3. You can get rid of a tapeworm by luring it out with a sausage held in front of your mouth.

HIT ? ☐ or MYTH ? ☐

The beef tapeworm doesn't even have a proper mouth, so to speak, so it couldn't gobble up a sausage, even if it wanted to. So this sausage fact is a myth-guided, myth-informed MYTH. Medicines, rather than sausages, give the tapeworm its marching orders.

4. Supermodels eat tapeworms to stay thin.

HIT ? ☐ or MYTH ? ☐

Another big, fat porky (although there is a pork tapeworm as well as the beef one!) The beef tapeworm does eat some of the food in our guts that oozes past it, but not that much, certainly not enough to make us supermodel-thin.

Because it doesn't have a mouth, it has to make do by absorbing some of our food through its skin. So, while it's true that it sucks some of the goodness from our food, it doesn't get huge feeds. In fact, incredibly for such an enormous worm, most beef tapeworms cause very few ill effects at all, perhaps just tummy pain and occasional nausea.

It seems that the supermodel tale is a story as tall as a beef tapeworm's tail is long!

The beef tapeworm – stuff of long tails, and tall tales!

Slithering out from your bottom . . .

So, now you know that a 10-metre-long worm can live inside us and not make us particularly sick. However, they do have one REALLY sick habit. Get this: sections of the tapeworm break off and come out of our bum, often in our poo, **but sometimes they wiggle out and slither down our thigh!**

The tapeworm's sections are special because they contain the worm's eggs. The reason they break off from the body of the worm and are pooed out of us (or slither out of our bottom and down our thigh) is so the eggs can get spread around, ready for a cow to eat. (Remember, this is a *beef* tapeworm.) This can happen in places where there aren't proper toilets. Inside the cow, the eggs hatch and make their way to the animal's muscles, where they live, waiting for us to eat the meat . . . so the whole cycle can start again.

HOLY COW!

The 'I've Got No Clue What Causes this Fever' Fever

Q fever (*Coxiella burnetii*)

How you pronounce it:
Cocks-ee-ella burr-net-ee

Pssst! I've got a secret for you. Most adults know a lot less than they make out. The sad, sorry truth is they spend a lot of their time pretending they are cleverer and more knowledgeable than they really are. (I should know, I am one . . . just.)

That's one reason why adults make up long words for things that could be explained much more simply. These complicated words are called *jargon*. The purpose of jargon is to make you sound clever. Doctors do it all the time; they have confusing words for lots of simple things.

For example, doctors say 'hypertension' when they mean 'high blood pressure'; and 'pyrexia' when they mean 'fever'. They call your bellybutton an 'umbilicus', the back of your head an 'occiput', and your bumcrack – WAIT FOR IT – the 'natal cleft'. 'Axilla' sounds clever, while 'armpit' sounds, well, like the pits. But they're both the same thing!

Doctor-speak is chock-a-block with jargon. Which is why a disease called Q fever is a refreshing change. Q fever sounds cool and sort of secretive. But it's not at all. All the Q stands for is 'query', as in 'question', as in 'I don't really know!'

Jargon gone

Like I said before, adults sometimes don't know all the answers.

And Dr Edward Derrick was left scratching his head when he investigated an outbreak of a strange illness among workers at a Brisbane meat processing factory in the 1930s. The clever Dr Derrick figured out that all the workers had the same illness – a mysterious type of fever – but he couldn't find the cause, so he just called it Query fever. And the refreshingly honest name, later shortened to Q fever, stuck. So Q fever really means 'I've got no clue what causes this fever' fever.

Doctored body parts

Here are some more simple things that doctors have complicated names for:

Thenar eminence
The smooth mound of muscle on our palm, just below our thumb.

Popliteal fossa
The shallow depression at the back of the knee.

Olecranon
The pointy, bony bit at the back of our elbow.

Masseter
The muscle in our jaw that that clenches our teeth.

In fact, there are many weird and wonderful names for our body parts, all with interesting stories behind them. Have a look for yourself on the net. Can you locate your Bundle of His, Islets of Langerhans, Circle of Willis, or even your Zonule of Zinn? How cool are they? Bet you didn't know you had 'em.

From poo to Q

Today, doctors know that Q fever is actually caused by the *Coxiella burnetii* bacteria. This bug lives in animals, such as kangaroos, cattle and sheep, and it comes out in their milk, wee and poo.

People often get Q fever when they breathe in the bug. But they don't breathe in sheep wee or poo – **that would be WEIRD**. They usually catch the bug by breathing in dust. When the poo in which this very tough little bacteria lives dries out and becomes dust, the bug can still survive in the particles for years. Then one day the wind might whip it up into the air and some poor person may breathe it in.

In Australia, meat and livestock workers are the people most likely to come down with Q fever, but there are medicines to fight the bug. People

If you haven't got a clue, go to Google

When some doctors are stumped by a difficult case, Google can help them work out the patient's problem. Researchers found that if you Google the symptoms of an illness, the search engine is quite good at finding the cause of the illness. This new research started after a father used Google to diagnose his son with something called Paget-von-Schrotter syndrome. (That's a problem caused by blocked veins!) Still confused? Google it for yourself!

in danger of infection can also get a vaccination to protect themselves, which doctors call a 'subcutaneous injection'. 'Subcutaneous' sounds nasty, but don't worry, it's just another example of doctor jargon – all it means is 'under the skin'!

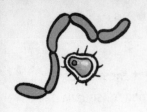

29

Malice in Wonderland

Epstein–Barr virus aka EBV

HOW YOU PRONOUNCE IT:

Ep-steen Bar vi-rus

The sun's streaming through your bedroom window, and you should have been up 15 minutes ago. Now mum's shouting, 'You'll be late for school, AGAIN!' But she hasn't done her Incredible Hulk impersonation and smashed your bedroom door down . . . yet. So you know you've got a minute or two longer to snuggle up. Yup, it's just another normal morning in your normal life . . .

But it's NOT a normal morning, because you notice something very creepy. Something that scares the living daylights out of you.

While you were sleeping, your neck has grown strangely long, just like a giraffe's. Your head is now perched high above your body – so high that you can look down and see that your arms have also been stretched. Your tiny hands are far away on the other side of the room!

You pinch yourself. You must be dreaming. But you're not, because that's your mum again, and now she's getting *really* cross. But she's suddenly the least of your worries. Now you're sick with fear from looking at your rubber-band body, and you can't control your panic. You start screaming . . .

Welcome to Wonderland!

This isn't a made-up story. It's a real illness. In fact, doctors have a great name for it: Alice in Wonderland syndrome. Though it's obviously not wonderful, it's certainly weird, and it's caused by a type of virus called EBV. Some viruses are a pain in the neck. This one can stretch your neck – strange!

Microbial mind games

When I said the story was real, that was absolutely true. What wasn't strictly true was the part about the kid's neck *actually* growing and his arms *actually* becoming massively stretched out like a long piece of week-old chewing gum. But that doesn't matter one bit. Why? Because to the poor boy in the story all these things *felt* completely real, as real as this book or a cricket ball flying over the boundary for six (cool) or the homework you have to do (uncool). And that's because his mind was playing tricks on him.

So that is what EBV can sometimes do – turn our minds against us. We may see and feel totally strange and outlandish things. Things that aren't really there, but seem like they are. For example, as well as feeling like their body has been strangely distorted,

STRANGE BODY DISTORTION FACT #1: China recently banned people from having operations to make their legs longer. They wanted to be taller because they thought greater height would help them get a better job. I'm not pulling your leg!

143

people with Alice in Wonderland syndrome can have experiences where objects seem to be much farther away (or closer) than they really are. Time can seem to run sluggishly slowly or frantically fast, or maybe things feel really odd to touch, like the ground may seem spongy. I think you'll have to agree all that is unspeakably freaky.

A really unreal story

Most of you would be familiar with the famous book *Alice's Adventures in Wonderland*, so it's probably no surprise that this bizarre illness and the bizarre story by Lewis Carroll are connected. In the book, lots of weird things happen to Alice's body and the things around her. Alice's 'out of this world' experiences are just the sorts of things people with Alice in Wonderland syndrome can feel. (Obviously doctors read great kids' books as well as thick, boring medical textbooks!)

A nutty adventure in a nutshell

First Alice chases a white rabbit down a seemingly endless hole. At the bottom there is a long passage that ends in a hall, where she finds a table with a key on it that opens a tiny door, but she is far too big to get through. Then she finds a bottle of potion, which she drinks, and it makes her shrink until she is 10 inches, or 25 centimetres high – small enough to go through the door. 'I must be shutting up like a telescope,' she says. Problem is, the key is still on the table, and she's too small to reach up to it and open the door. She finds a cake, which she also eats, and this time it makes her grow to more than 9 feet, or 2.7 metres high. 'Now I'm opening out like the largest telescope that ever was!' she says. 'Good-bye, feet! Oh, my poor little feet, I wonder who will put on your shoes and stockings for you now, dears?' she cries.

Have you ever got off a
boat or a plane and felt like
you were still rocking and
pitching around, even
though you were on solid
ground? Doctors have a
French name for this
temporary feeling: mal de
debarquement. Sounds
fancy schmancy for an
illness!

EBV: Keep it real dude

Get this – EBV is incredibly common, pretty much everyone gets it. But luckily most of the time this tiny virus keeps its creepy closet of horrors under lock and key. Often it's really quite a dull bug. It usually causes an illness called glandular fever, which makes us feel worn out, rather than freaked out.

The ABC on EBV

A. EBV: real name, Epstein-Barr virus. It is named after Michael Epstein and Yvonne Barr, who (with Bert Achong) first found the virus in 1964.

B. Usually travels from one person to the next in their spit. This means you can get it when you share spit (ewww!), like when you kiss someone, or use someone else's drinking straw or toothbrush.

C. Usually causes an illness called glandular fever, which is also known as the 'kissing disease'; young people who have 'lashings of pashing' can get it. People with glandular fever often have a fever (naturally), a sore throat and feel like they have no energy, like a battery that's run out of juice. It can take months to get over it.

EBV only gives people Alice in Wonderland syndrome very rarely, and, when it does, the horrible illusions and feelings usually go away on their own reasonably quickly. Which is great, unless you'd like your world to be totally mixed up, stretched out, spun around and turned on its head – even if it's only all in your head!

A Toe-tally Sick Day at the Beach

Sand flea or jigger (*Tunga penetrans*)

HOW YOU PRONOUNCE IT:

Tunn-gar pen-uh-trans

When you come home from a trip to the beach, just about the nastiest, most uncomfortable thing you'll ever find stuck between your toes is sand. But what if you dusted off your thongs on the front porch, and there, nestled between your dirty digits, was something much more sinister. Something ALIVE! Something that was burrowing into your skin so it could make its home inside you. Something that was greedily sucking your blood and laying its eggs.

> FLEA! FI! FO! FUM! I SMELL THE **BLOOD** OF AN AUSTRALIAN.

> BE SHE ALIVE OR BE SHE **DEAD**, I'LL SUCK HER BLOOD TO MAKE ME **FED**.

Enough of the 'somethings' and the 'what ifs', because some doctors are worried that this toe-tally sick scenario could happen if a particular little critter called a jigger manages to make Australia its home. If jiggers do get a firm foothold here, then they'll desperately try to get a firm hold of your feet, because that's where they like to live.

Jumping feats onto your feet

A jigger is a type of flea that likes to live in the dirt and sand – beaches suit it down to the ground. But they are in fact quite weedy fleas, in the freaky flea fraternity. At about 1 millimetre long, it is the smallest type of flea. And while most fleas are known for their excellent jumping prowess (they don't have wings), jiggers really aren't very good leapers.

Mighty flea feats
- Some fleas can jump 150 times their own length. If we could leap like fleas, we'd be able to hurdle 100-storey skyscrapers.
- A hungry flea can jump 10,000 times in an hour.
- Female fleas can eat 15 times their own body weight in blood a day.

*One giant leap
for flea-kind.*

That's the reason jiggers often end up on people's toes and feet – they simply can't jump any higher to reach bits of you further up. While jiggers won't get a medal in the high jump at the Flea Olympics, they do stand a better chance of winning 'Gold, Gold, Gold' in the blood-sucking championships. They survive on the warm red juice that keeps us alive, and that's especially so for female jiggers when they need to make babies.

After male and female jiggers have 'jiggied' together and mated, the female has to lay her eggs. And she accomplishes this by finding you, or another warm-blooded animal like a dog or a cat, and burrowing headfirst into your skin until she finds some blood vessels to tap into. And there she sits, **happy as a pig in mud** (or, rather, a flea in blood) with her head down and her bottom sticking out from the skin between your toes. She then lays a hundred or so of her precious eggs, which easily end up out in the dirt beneath your feet and soon these small, white fleas-to-be hatch. The babies thrive in dust and sand, and in a few weeks they become adult fleas, all ready to mate and feed off you and your friends all over again.

One small step for man, one giant leap for flea-kind

The good news, at least for Australians, is that jiggers are common overseas, particularly in Africa, but not here. For now. The bad news is that, not long ago, doctors found jiggers in some children in Sydney. It turns out these resourceful little ankle-biters had travelled all the way from Africa to the Lucky Country.

So how on earth could a feeble flea that can't jump very far, compared with its other flea friends, make the giant leap across continents? The answer has wings rather than legs and guzzles aviation fuel rather than blood: a jet plane!

Question: What do you call a jigger that catches a plane all the way from Africa to Australia? Answer: A *flea*quent flyer!

These jiggers had hitched a ride inside the toes and feet of some children who had taken a flight here from Africa. The kids had been living in crowded refugee camps in a poor country called Tanzania.

Jiggery pokery that really hurts

Two hundred years ago, German explorer Hans Meyer saw the terrible hurt jiggers can inflict in Africa. Travelling through Tanzania, Dr Meyer called jiggers 'the most fearful calamity that has ever afflicted the East African peoples'. And he wrote about people with the embedded fleas who couldn't walk and had to crawl around on all fours, groaning.

Their doctors in Sydney found small, pale-yellow nodules on their feet, mainly on their toes and between them. The nodules where the female jiggers had burrowed were painful and itchy. (Usually that's about as harmful as jiggers get, unless bacteria come along and infect where the jiggers have set up shop. Then those new microbes can cause a serious infection.) The kids' toes also had tiny things that looked like seeds on them, and these were the jiggers' eggs – which isn't 'eggs-actly' very pleasant.

Because of all this, the doctors who saw the children were worried that jiggers might eventually settle here if more and more people brought them into the country in their feet and toes. And that, I reckon, would be 'dread-flea' toe-curling.

Rubber that's the flea's knees

Aussie scientists have made a type of rubber from a cool chemical called resilin that gives fleas their amazing jumping prowess. The rubber could perhaps be used to make running shoes super-springy.

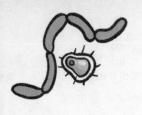

Rat Attack Bite Fright

Rat–bite fever (*Streptobacillus moniliformis* and *Spirillum minus*)

Strep-toe-baa-sill-us mon-ill-ee-form-iss
Spy-rill-um mine-us

How can you catch rat-bite fever? Is it from a) dog bites? b) rat bites? or c) your sister? Dumb question or WHAT?! Don't think you'll need to strain your brain on this one!

Rat-bite fever can be deadly, and you get it after a bite from a . . . rat! Nothing surprising about that. But what is amazing is that the disease isn't more common, because rats are *amazingly* common.

You might not see these ghastly, gnawing rodents every day, but they are always nearby, scurrying down below the streets in the sewers, and rustling around rubbish in dark cellars and dingy basements. These rodent low-lifes are just like girlfriends and boyfriends in

A rat for every person.

a way: the scary truth is that there is one out there for each of us. (What's more scary, rats or girlfriends and boyfriends?)

So, when the American government wants to work out how many rats live in a city (why, I've no idea) it assumes **there is one rat for every person**. But luckily rats aren't big-time biters, because they can carry the bacteria that cause rate-bite fever. This disease can kill around one in ten people who don't get the right medicines. Common symptoms include: fever – obviously! – chills, spewing and painful joints. Depending on the rat's nationality, it's caused by two different bacteria: in America by *Streptobacillus moniliformis* and in Africa and Asia by *Spirillum minus*.

But rat bites aren't the only way to get rat-bite fever – rats only need to scratch you to transmit the bug, or poo on your food without you knowing, so make sure those raisins in your breakfast cereal aren't rat pellets! Yuck!

Rat attack facts

In New York City in 1996, there were 184 reports of people getting bitten by a rat. Which is a tiny amount when you consider that in the same year about 1,100 people in the city said they'd been bitten by another person! And a whopping 10,000 or so suffered dog bites.

Aussie doctors have also identified another way of catching rat-bite fever, because they found the bacteria in someone who had been bitten . . . by a dog! The polluted pup was a greyhound – a breed that eats animals like the bacteria-carrying rats.

So, maybe the question at the beginning of this story wasn't so dumb after all! (Not sure about your sister though.)

A disease, not a puzzle: in Japan rat-bite fever is known as sodoku – almost the same as the popular number game sudoku!

Worm Alert! Attention All Bum-scratchers!

Threadworm (*Enterobius vermicularis*)

En-ter-oh-bee-us ver-mick-you-lar-iss

You may not have seen a threadworm, or even heard of it, even though it's very common among kids like you – almost all of us get infested with it at some time in our lives. But you've probably *felt* a threadworm (or three) in a very dark and private place. No, I'm not talking about the space under your bed – **I'm referring to your bumhole!**

These critters like to party around the entrance to your bumhole, crawling about, laying their eggs and making your bottom ickily itchy. But this irritating tickling doesn't happen by accident, it's all part of the worm's plan to trick you into eating it – that's the unpalatable truth of this story.

SCRATCH
SKRITCH
SCRATCH!!

What's that you cry? 'Me? Conned by a squirming little bumhole worm? That can't be!' Well it can be – this itchy little wriggler will have you really squirming in your seat, because it's a lot cleverer than you might think.

Think I'm going to eat worms . . .

The reason why threadworms want us to eat them has everything to do with their lifestyle – surfing and beach cricket just don't cut it for 'em. A threadworm's life is still pretty good. These 1-centimetre-long worms actually make their home inside your warm intestines. While there might not be that much to do inside your guts – it's bottom-bendingly boring – it is safe and there's lots of food for them (the food you eat) flowing past.

But things get more interesting in your intestine when the worms make babies. The female worms fill up with eggs, which she has to lay on the outside of you (rather than inside your guts). The 'outside' means where your intestines open to the outside world: your bumhole! This journey from inside your gut to outside your butt is important because if the female threadworm **just spilled her eggs into your intestine**, they wouldn't be very likely to infect another person, or you. The eggs would end up going the way of all your poo: out of your bum to be flushed away down the loo, not into someone else.

So, she takes a trip downstream through your guts. And, late at night, when you are in bed, she wriggles out of your bottom into the outside world. And there, around your bumhole, she lays loads of her precious eggs, before quickly nipping back into the safety of your back passage.

Mission accomplished! Although there is still one very big problem to overcome: for the eggs to grow into adult worms and infect you properly, they have to somehow get to your mouth so you can swallow them into your guts again. You see, the eggs can only hatch much higher up in your guts than where the worms usually live. And this 'hatchery' is not that far down the digestive tract from your mouth. So, just how do these sneaky, creepy little creatures get all the way from your bottom up to your mouth?

Why are they called threadworms?

They are worms and they look like a small piece of white thread, obviously. If you wanted to sound clever, you could use the name scientific experts have for them: *Enterobius vermicularis*. But then nobody would have any clue what you were talking about . . . show-off!

Tricking you into giving a helping hand

So, pretend you're a tiny, defenceless worm egg stuck on some kid's butt, and you have got to get all the way to the snotty little child's mouth. It's like the reality TV show *The Amazing Race*. The one where people have to race around the world following clues and working out the best route to get to the next destination: you have two possible routes, each with its own pros and cons! Which one should you choose?

Threadworms are very contagious critters because their eggs can survive for weeks outside the body, like on your bedclothes, and can spread through the air and into our mouths. An 'air-raising' thought.

ROUTE #1: Marathon madness. You could swim up the river of the kid's intestines, fighting against the flow of the constant stream of poo. That marathon swim might be too tricky for tiny little you.

ROUTE #2: Overland adventure. You could set off from the kid's bumhole and travel 'overland' on their skin. This means wriggling up their bumcrack, over their back, onto their shoulder, then up their neck and cheek and, finally, into their mouth. It's not as long a trip as the marathon swim, but taking the overland trek would leave you perilously exposed.

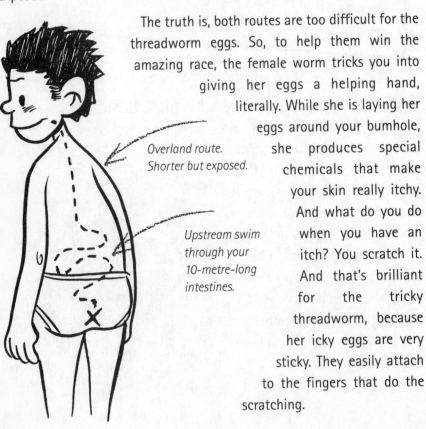

Overland route. Shorter but exposed.

Upstream swim through your 10-metre-long intestines.

The truth is, both routes are too difficult for the threadworm eggs. So, to help them win the amazing race, the female worm tricks you into giving her eggs a helping hand, literally. While she is laying her eggs around your bumhole, she produces special chemicals that make your skin really itchy. And what do you do when you have an itch? You scratch it. And that's brilliant for the tricky threadworm, because her icky eggs are very sticky. They easily attach to the fingers that do the scratching.

All the threadworm has to do now is wait for the kid to put his (or her – girls scratch their bums too!) fingers in his mouth. If he's chewing his nails or sucking his thumb, the worm eggs go straight into his mouth too. So the kid swallows the eggs, allowing them to travel back down into his guts, where they'll grow up and live happily . . . until *their* babies have to go on the dangerous amazing race again.

Giving threadworms some stick

Sometimes people use sticky tape to tell if a kid has threadworms! They put the tape onto the skin around the kid's bumhole, so any eggs there will stick to it. Then they look at the tape under a microscope for the eggs. There are medicines that get rid of these wretched wrigglers, but it's also important to avoid getting infected by doing things like washing your hands before meals and after going to the toilet . . . but you already knew that.

33

The Strange Case of the Toxic Soccer Boots

Golden staph (*Staphylococcus aureus*)

How you pronounce it:
Staff-ill-oh-cock-us awe-ree-us

What's a new pair of soccer boots for? Sticking the ball in the back of the net, that's what. GOOOOOOOOOOOOOAL! If you watched the Socceroos do so well at the 2006 World Cup in Germany, you'll know exactly what I'm talking about. Soccer fever (real name: FOOTBALL fever) swept through Australia and the rest of the world.

But for one unfortunate girl in England, soccer fever wasn't so exciting. In fact, she caught a dose of soccer fever that left her seriously ill in hospital, and could even have killed her. And it all started with a shiny new pair of soccer boots . . .

Flashback to the Soccer World Cup, June 2006

Just as the World Cup was starting and the best players on the planet were strapping on their footy boots, ready for action, doctors in England sent out a warning about the dangers of new soccer boots – and a special type of vicious bug. The alert came after the doctors had seen a girl who had played a game in her shiny new boots. She had come down with a fever straight away after the game and had a really bad skin rash over her tummy, arms and legs (plus lots of other nasty symptoms).

She was rushed off to hospital where doctors gave her medicines, hoping to sock it to whatever bugs were making the soccer player so gravely ill. But the girl didn't recover. **In fact, she quickly grew worse.** The doctors couldn't identify what was actually causing her nasty illness, so they weren't giving her the ideal medicines. (Believe it or not, doctors aren't *always* right.)

Perhaps the reason why the doctors hadn't spotted what was causing her mysterious illness was that they didn't know she had just played soccer in a new pair of boots. And perhaps they didn't know, or were too old to remember, what new soccer boots often do to your feet.

QUESTION: When new boots rub too much on your skin, what painful, annoying things can they cause?

ANSWER: Yes, blisters! If you knew that, then you are doing better than the doctors, who hadn't spotted that the girl's football fanatic antics had given her a big blister on each heel. They'd missed 'er blisters!

HALF-TIME: Staphylococcus aureus 1 – Doctors 0.

It was only after she'd been in hospital for a few days that an eagle-eyed medic spotted the nasty sores. And there inside the blisters, was something called pus – skanky, yellow-white gunk, caused by bacteria, which can ooze and squirt from wounds and zits and boils. And floating inside the pus was a type of bacteria called *Staphylococcus aureus*. This bug is often called golden staph, because when doctors grow it in laboratories, it can look golden.

It turned out that this pus-producing bug that was hidden away in the blisters on her feet had been causing her illness all along.

Nosing around golden staph

This is a bug that can really get up your nose. Literally, right up your nose, because lots of people who are quite well have golden staph bugs living in their noses without them doing much harm. But this bug can also cause lots of illnesses. Some are minor, like pimples, and some very serious. The girl in this story had one of the bad 'uns: something called toxic shock syndrome.

SFA (Strange Fact Alert): toxic shock syndrome can cause the skin on people's hands and feet to peel off, which is certainly not very appealing!

That's gold!
'Aureus' actually means 'gold' in Latin. That's why the chemical symbol for gold is Au.

The name toxic shock syndrome makes it sound as serious as it actually is: toxically shocking. About 5 per cent of kids who get the syndrome die – so, if 22 junior soccer players fall ill, one will get a red card and be sent off to the changing rooms in the sky. But the good news is that the syndrome is quite rare, so there is no need to hang up your soccer boots (new or old)!

But the girl in this story was lucky. After the doctors found her blisters, and the golden staph bugs in them, they were able to give her the right type of bacteria-busting medicines (antibiotics), and she soon got better.

So, fortunately this case of toxic bugs, blisters and soccer boots turned out okay, but only after the doctors had really given the golden staph bacteria the boot!

FULL-TIME: Staphylococcus aureus 1 – Doctors 2.

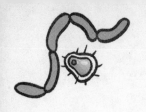

34

The Modest Little Page of the Oddest Big Fears

If you are scared to bits or out of your wits by the super gross-outs in this super bug book, maybe you've got a phobia? That's a massive, chest-tightening fear or heart-pumping panic over something that might not be terrifying enough to make 'normal people' freak out. **Phobias can really mess up people's lives**, because they can go to great lengths to avoid their fear. Of course, we *all* try to avoid fear, but if you have a strange, humungous dread of, say, open spaces like sports ovals, or confined spaces like showers, it's easy to see how that could really stuff up your life. Playing footy and having a wash after might be a tad tricky, eh, Pongster?

Or maybe you haven't got a phobia? Maybe your fears are simply those of a normal boy or girl? After all, who in their right mind wouldn't be terrified of catching cholera, which can give them diarrhoea gushing from their bum like a waterfall? Who isn't petrified of a 10-metre-long tapeworm camped out in their guts, or horrified by a bug that has their brain at the top of its list of yummy foods? Who wouldn't be mortified by any of the other nasties in this book?

So, now that we've established that you are probably normal, here are the names of some strange bug phobias you probably *don't* have. (Note: everyone is a little bit weird, especially you, the reader with the collection of dried-up bogeys stuck to the leg of your bedside table. **You know who you are!**)

SPERMATOPHOBIA	Fear of germs
IATROPHOBIA	Fear of going to the doctor
BACTERIOPHOBIA	Fear of bacteria
PEDICULOPHOBIA	Fear of lice
PARASITOPHOBIA	Fear of parasites
NOSOPHOBIA	Fear of getting ill
HELMINTHOPHOBIA	Fear of getting worms

But if you thought they were odd, here are some really far-out phobias:

DIDASKALEINOPHOBIA	Fear of going to school
BUFONOPHOBIA	Fear of toads
GENIOPHOBIA	Fear of chins
LOGOPHOBIA	Fear of words

HEXAKOSIOIHEXEKONTAHEXAPHOBIA Fear of the number 666, which is said to be the devil's number. Apparently Ronald Reagan, who was once President of the United States, didn't want to move into a house with the number 666, so he got it changed to 668. Presidents can do that sort of thing.

But these fears are nothing compared with this last one, which is way off the scale of strangeness:

ARACHIBUTYROPHOBIA That's fear of peanut butter sticking to the roof of your mouth. That's a little nutty if you ask me!

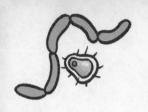

35

The 'Glowdown' on Weird Wounds

Photorhabdus

HOW YOU PRONOUNCE IT:
Foe-tor-hab-duhs

You know how cuts, wounds and skin sores can drip blood and ooze and weep and smart and sting and burn and throb and crust over and scab and sometimes can even get infected and drip nasty, gooey yellow pus? Don't you just hate it when that happens? But can you remember or imagine a sore that glows in the dark?

Well, strike a light, they can . . . if they are caused by an incredible rod-shaped Aussie bug called *Photorhabdus*. This unique bacteria has a very special power indeed. It uses chemicals in its body to make light, and

166

The east coast of Australia is good to glow, thanks to Photorhabdus, *which literally means 'glowing rods'.*

it's the only bacteria living on land that can perform this remarkable glowing trick called bioluminescence.

When people get a skin problem, medicos usually look at it under a bright light to help work out what's going on, but to diagnose this strange bug, you need to do the complete opposite. You have to turn off all the lights and look out for an eerie, blue-white glow!

Glow, Aussie, glow!

Another strange thing about this bug is that it's only been found to infect people in a few places in the world: the US (mostly in Texas), Nepal and the east coast of Australia. So, if you have a sore on your skin, why not turn out the lights, take ten minutes or so for your eyes to adjust to the darkness and, you never know, perhaps you'll be in for a weird *Photorhabdus* glow show?

Although after reading this you'll probably be hoping for a 'glow show no show' and be happy just to sit around in the dark, because the type of *Photorhabdus* that infects people can cause very nasty skin sores. Often these ugly sores are on their feet, and they are more common in warm, wet weather, especially after heavy rainstorms.

The word 'bioluminescence' comes from the Greek for 'living' (bios) and the Latin for 'light' (lumen).

Glowing bugs and worm warfare

But infecting humans is really only something this bug does in its spare time. After all, there have only been about 15 people in the world who have been known to have fallen ill with it. (Experts think it's probably much more common, but doctors don't often spot it, or mistake it for better-known bugs.)

It's likely that the bacteria's real job is to help grubby little worms kill insects! Insects make a great meal for *Photorhabdus* and the worms. We probably get infected with *Photorhabdus* from the soil, but the bug can't survive on its own in the dirt. It must live inside another animal there, perhaps tiny worms (less than 1 millimetre long) that are common in soil. And these worms use the glowing bugs to kill insects like caterpillar larvae.

And here's the glowdown, er, I mean *lowdown*, on how the glowing bacteria–worm combo probably does it. The clever worms worm their way into the caterpillar larva and let the bacteria loose inside the insect. The even cleverer bacteria make strong

The glow in the oceans

Lots of animals in the oceans use bioluminescence to make light. Anglerfish have an appendage like a fishing rod attached to their foreheads that has a glowing lure on the tip to attract prey. And cookiecutter sharks use bioluminescence for camouflage. They have a dark body with just a small patch of glowing skin, which makes them look like they are tiny – just a patch of light – to other fish. Glowing sea bacteria use this power for communication and to help them infect hosts.

chemicals that kill the insect. When the poor caterpillar larva is dead, the bacteria climb back into the worm, and the cool killing combo moves on to slay another insect. It really is a case of germ – and worm – warfare!

But why do these bacteria actually need to make light? No one knows for sure, but the theory goes like this: When the caterpillar larva is dead, the bacteria glow. And what do lots of insects do when they see light? They go straight for the glow, like when insects busily buzz around an outdoor lamp at night. These crafty bacteria are like little microbial light bulbs, and when the insects gather, the bug–worm combo is waiting for the kill.

Photorhabdus is surely a shining example of the amazing powers of the bug world.

Strange tales of 'angel glow'

Throughout history there have been odd stories of soldiers on the battlefield suffering from strange wounds that glow in the dark. No one knows if this weird phenomenon, called 'angel glow', is real or just a myth. But some people think angel glow can happen and the *Photorhabdus* bug is the cause.

The mystery of the milky sea

For centuries, sailors have talked about a mysterious milky white glow that sometimes appears on the ocean's surface. Often it was dismissed as the sailors' eyes playing tricks on them, or just fishermen's tales, until a space satellite took a picture of a big, glowing patch of water in the Indian Ocean. It's thought that bacteria were responsible for this strange sight.

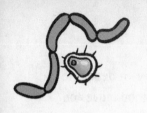

36

TB Alive or TB Dead (or Undead . . .)

Tuberculosis (*Mycobacterium tuberculosis*)

HOW YOU PRONOUNCE IT:

My-co-back-teer-ee-um tue-ber-que-low-sis

Mercy Brown definitely wasn't a vampire. She was just a little girl who died of a horrible illness called TB. So why did her father dig her lifeless body out of the ground, cut out her heart and feed it to her brother because he was convinced Mary was actually a vampire? Why did the father believe Mary had cursed his boy?

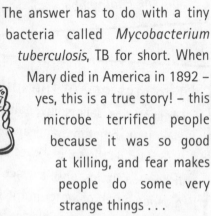

The answer has to do with a tiny bacteria called *Mycobacterium tuberculosis*, TB for short. When Mary died in America in 1892 – yes, this is a true story! – this microbe terrified people because it was so good at killing, and fear makes people do some very strange things . . .

TB easily spreads in

the air through coughs and sneezes, so it can quickly jump from person to person, especially when the people live together, like members of the same family. Sadly, that's what befell the Brown family: first Mary's mum died of TB, then her elder sister and, finally, Mary. And it just so happened that Mary's father, George Brown, believed that if lots of people in the same family died, vampires – the 'UNDEAD' – were responsible! TB can cause a bad lung disease, in which people have fever, weight loss and can cough up blood. It can seem like the life is being drained right from them. That's why people like George Brown believed the disease was caused by dead people returning from the grave and sucking the life out of the living! (At the time scientists knew little about bugs and how diseases were caused.)

Coffins and coughin'

Ordinary people often had only strange, traditional remedies to rely on, which is what George Brown did when his son Edwin also became terribly sick with TB after Mary's death. George persuaded friends to help him dig up the bodies of his wife and two daughters to see if one of them wasn't dead at all – maybe one was 'undead' and would suck the life out of Edwin and the rest of the family. After all, Edwin was coughing his way to his coffin, too.

When George did the grisly business of opening the coffins, he found his wife's and first daughter's body had **horribly rotted away** – they had been dead for *four* years. But, surprise, surprise, the recently dead body of Mary was still almost intact. And that was a sign that she lived beyond death! A sign that Mary was actually draining young Edwin's life away.

So, the remedy was simple: rip the cold, still heart from Mary's corpse, burn it, mix the ashes with water and give it to Edwin to drink! Of corpse! A hearty remedy if ever there was one! So, what do you think happened to poor Edwin? Did he make a miraculous recovery because his undead, vampire sister had been finally vanquished? Or did he drink disgusting ashes mixed with water, puke it up, cough up some blood and die a horrible death from TB a month or so later? I think you know the answer . . .

Tsunamis and billionaires (but no vampires!)

Sadly, we still don't have the answer to TB, because it's one of the most bug-bogglingly big health problems on Earth. Think about this: the tiny TB bug can make a disastrous tsunami seem like a little ripple and a billionaire seem a little less like a mega moneybags!

TB kills someone every 15 seconds.

TB infects about one in three of ALL the people in the world today, and it kills millions upon millions. Luckily, most people who get infected don't actually get sick, and the bug lies in a dormant, sleeping state. But if their protective immune system is weakened, by them not having enough to eat for example, they are more likely to get ill. That's why poverty helps TB thrive and the illness is common in poor countries in Africa and Southeast Asia. Every second that ticks by, someone is infected with TB, and every 15 seconds this bug kills a person.

In Australia, there are about 1000 TB cases a year, mainly in people born overseas.

According to that figure, maybe 4 or 5 people have died of TB since you started reading this story. And the sad truth is that there are medicines to treat it and vaccines to help prevent it. Scary, isn't it?

The tsunami you *haven't* heard of

The world's massive TB disaster certainly puts catastrophes like the 2004 Boxing Day tsunami into perspective. That terrible Asian tsunami killed hundreds of thousands of people, and you probably remember from the news how almost immediately countries like Australia started giving help to the victims.

But, not long after, a doctor here pointed out that every year in the region where the tsunami hit, the number of people killed by TB is 2-3 times *more* than the number of victims of that giant wave. He called it 'the tsunami of TB', and the tragedy is that it goes almost unnoticed!

The doctor said more should be done around the world about TB, and in 2006 a big worldwide plan, called 'The Global Plan to Stop TB', started up to try and put the brakes on the bug.

The billion dollar drop in the ocean

To kick-start the effort to kick TB into touch, Bill Gates – that gazillionaire computer whiz kid and all-round good guy – donated almost $1 billion US dollars. Ka-ching! Even though the  donation was mega generous, it's unfortunately only a drop in the ocean in the fight against TB. That's because the The Global Plan to Stop TB needs at least $56 BILLION US dollars over the next 10 years if it's going to do what it aims to do, which is to save 14 million people's lives.

So the plan needs rich people and governments around the world to rummage round their pockets and stump up some loose change. It will change the world, TB sure!

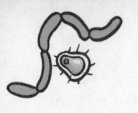

The Fiery Serpent,
the Cyclops and
the Amazingly Clever Trick

Guinea worm *(Dracunculus medinensis)*

HOW YOU PRONOUNCE IT:

Dra-coon-cool-us medin-en-sis

Gives new meaning to the phrase 'I jumped out of my skin'.

Prepare to come face-to-face with a giant serpent that creeps silently through your insides before bursting out of your skin in a horribly painful spasm. And get ready to befriend a tiny fiend called Cyclops that dissolves away in your intestines, releasing lots and lots of baby worms into your guts.

Look up horrible in the dictionary and you'll find the serpent's scientific name: *Dracunculus medinensis*. Its common name is the Guinea worm, and when the Bible was written (that's a long, long time ago) it was called the 'fiery serpent'.

Read on, if you dare, because this is a story full of terrible suffering, brilliant trickery, and, oh yes, a gut full of worms.

The serpent

The adult Guinea worm is as thin as a piece of string and almost as long as a cricket bat (80 centimetres long for those of you who are particular about these things). This frightening fact makes it perhaps the largest parasite that lives inside human flesh. (Tapeworms can be longer but they live inside the tube of our guts, not burrowed in our flesh). But when the Guinea worm is young it's very tiny, so tiny that we can drink it up in water without even knowing. And that's the secret to how it spreads from person to person - through contaminated drinking water.

The Guinea worm is especially common in Sudan, the largest country in Africa, where many people have nothing but dirty water to drink. And if they are unlucky enough to have a cup of contaminated water, the bug washes into their intestines, along with all the churned-up food

Sudan, home of the Guinea worm. **Travel Tip:** *avoid the Cyclops flea soup.*

and drink they have eaten – yuk! But worms don't mind yuk; they are worms after all. Once in the 'goo that's about to become poo', they make an exit, burrowing through the lining of our guts and into the surrounding flesh.

Human flesh: that's where guinea worms call home, grow up and fall in love. It's warm; it's cosy – I guess they could do worse. Good lovin' for a Guinea worm means rummaging though a living human body to find a worm of the opposite sex and making babies. And then, if you're the guy worm, you die. That's romance worm style.

You see, the female worm doesn't need the guy

According to the United Nations, unclean water is a greater threat to people in the world than wars.

worm any more, now that she is pregnant with hundreds of thousands of baby worms (called larvae). The grim fact is that kids are more important than boyfriends, at least in the world of the Guinea worm.

With the babies inside her, the Guinea worm slithers through the body, down towards the legs. Usually, all this slithering happens without the poor person who is infected knowing anything about it. But, after a year or so, things turn NASTY.

Dead Guinea worms have been found in ancient Egyptian mummies!

The agony and the trickery

Just how would you feel if an 80-centimetre-long worm suddenly emerged out of your foot? It's pretty horrible. No, it's SUPER, MEGA HORRIBLE. But what makes this gory experience worse is that it is also heaps painful. But it's no ordinary pain; the fiery serpent causes a special burning type of pain. And this is how the Guinea worm tricks us.

What do people do when they burn themselves? They often go to water to soothe the burn. And the Guinea worm needs water, because that's where she has to deposit her babies so they'll survive. Problem is, when the Guinea worms emerge from our skin, we are usually on dry land.

Getting you into the water is a matter of life and death for the Guinea worm babies. So, as the mother's coming out of your foot, she makes you feel like your leg is on fire, and you jump in the water. And, right at that moment, she chucks her babies safely into the water. The Guinea worm: more tortuous than a serpent that is good at torturing; cleverer than a very clever thing.

The Cyclops

This explains how the Guinea worm larvae get into the water we drink, but they now need a way of surviving in the water. They do this with the help of a hungry little animal called a Cyclops. In ancient mythology the Cyclops was a giant monster with only one eye, but these Cyclopses are tiny things:

Giant, one-eyed Cyclops, the stuff of legend.

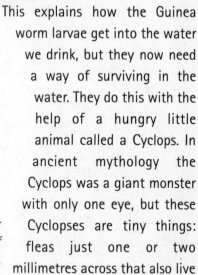

Tiny Cyclops water flea, likes the taste of guinea worm babies.

fleas just one or two millimetres across that also live in the contaminated water. And guess what they call Guinea worm babies? **They call them lunch.**

You'd think that being spewed out of their mum into water and becoming a Cyclops flea's meal would kill the Guinea worm babies. 'Course it doesn't. These critters ain't no quitters. The Guinea worm babies thrive inside the fleas.

And the Cyclops flea is the secret to how the Guinea worm gets into us without being noticed – it simply hitches a ride inside the small fleas! In poor countries that can't treat their water against bugs, the fleas can easily get mixed into the drinking water, ready for some unsuspecting, thirsty victim to have a sip. Little does he know that there are Cyclops fleas in the water, and inside the Cyclops fleas there are Guinea worm babies that are ready to burst out into his intestines.

And now we're back to where this whole story began. This is certainly a tale with a nasty sting in its tail.

The life and times of the Guinea worm, alias the fiery serpent

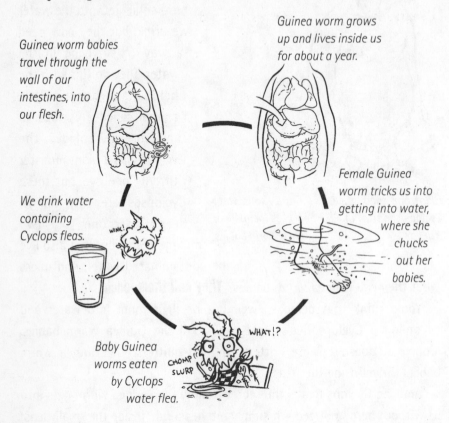

Guinea worm babies travel through the wall of our intestines, into our flesh.

Guinea worm grows up and lives inside us for about a year.

We drink water containing Cyclops fleas.

WINK!

Female Guinea worm tricks us into getting into water, where she chucks out her babies.

Baby Guinea worms eaten by Cyclops water flea.

CHOMP SLURP

WHAT!?

A final twist

A good way of removing the worm as it comes out of your foot (which is where it emerges from 90 per cent of the time) is to wrap it around a wooden stick, which you then twist so the worm slowly winds from the festering hole in the skin. This may be the origin of the famous old symbol for medicine and doctors: a one-headed snake wrapped around a stick!

Puzzles to Bug Your Brain #1: The Riddle of the Sands

Can you solve the riddle of the sands and get the better of a nasty bug that you'll find lurking in this book? To outwit the bug, you have to work out what each of the six letters is, from 1st to 6th, that spell the bug's name.

HINT: when I say my first letter is in 'major' but not in 'order', that means the first letter of this bug's name is contained in the word 'major', but you won't find it in the word 'order'. So the first letter is either 'm', 'a' or 'j'.

My first letter is in 'major' but not in 'order'.   1st

My second letter is in 'growing' but not in 'grow'.   2nd

My third letter is in 'leg' but not in 'leap'.   3rd

My fourth letter is in 'slag' but not in 'heap'.   4th

My fifth letter is in 'eagle' but not in 'gull'.   5th

My sixth letter is in 'rudder' but not in 'hull'.   6th

And my whole is in sand, but I'd like to be in you! Who am I? (If you're stuck, the answer is on page 186, and it also lives in chapter 30.)

Puzzles to Bug Your Brain #2: The Da Bacteria Code

Can you crack the Da Bacteria Code? It's vitally important that you do, because a young girl is very ill. And the message written below in code tells you what's wrong with her and what she needs to make her better. Hurry, you've only got **10 minutes** to save her!

In the code, the letters for words have been jumbled up, so you'll need to use the special decoder grid to solve it. HURRY, a life is at stake! Your time starts . . . now!

```
____  ____  ____  ___  _  ____  ___  _
TYHQ  SEEA  UHAF  YPQ  P  JICIA  PDK  P

_____  ___  ____  ____  ____  ___
AIPFFN  LAK  QTHD  APQY  ECIA  YIA

_____,  ____  ___  ____  ____  ____
ZXRRN,  PARQ  PDK  FIUQ  SFXQ  FEZQ

__  _____  _____  _____.  ___  ___
EJ  EZYIA  DPQZN  QNRSZERQ.  QYI  YPQ

_____  _____  _____  _____  __
TEBHO  QYEOT  QNDKAERI  OPXQIK  LN

_____  _____  _____.  ___
QZPSYNFEOEOOXQ  PXAIXQ  LPOZIAHP.  QYI

____  _____  _____  _____.
BIIKQ  RIKHOHDIQ  OPFFIK  PDZHLHEZHOQ.
```

DECODER GRID

Actual letter	Code letter
A	P
B	L
C	O
D	K
E	I
F	J
G	U
H	Y
I	H
J	G
K	T
L	F
M	R
N	D
O	E
P	S
Q	W
R	A
S	Q
T	Z
U	X
V	C
W	V
X	B
Y	N
Z	M

So, what illness does the girl have? What does she need to make her better? And, most importantly, did you figure it out and save her in time?

(The cure is on page 186.)

Puzzles to Bug Your Brain #3: Scrambled Bugs

Yuor barin is mcuh mroe pwruefol tahn you tinhk!

Did you rlsieae taht if you mix wdros up, but lavee the fsirt and lsat lretets in tiehr rgiht pacle, you can slitl raed tehm, wtih a bit of erofft? Anzimag!

Hree are smoe bug wdros mtenienod in tihs book taht hvae been mexid up in tihs way.

Can you wrok out waht tehy are?

1. Wtras
2. Fveer
3. Jgegir
4. Twraopem
5. Vruis
6. Gnagnere
7. Fnuugs
8. Husoe dsut mtie
9. Gnieua wrom
10. Speinelg sknicess

(Answers on page 186.)

Puzzles to Bug Your Brain #4: Enter the Microbial MATRIX

Inside this Matrix are 15 names of bugs or illnesses in this book. The names go across or down, but not diagonally, can you spot them? Here is a list of the things you are trying to spot: *Plague, Flu, Q fever, Bacteria, HIV, Head lice, MRSA, E. coli, Cholera, Virus, Malaria, EBV, Fungus, TB* and *Ebola*.

A	S	H	I	V	E	R	A	Q	U
L	H	I	N	I	T	B	N	F	N
M	A	L	A	R	I	A	E	E	R
F	U	N	G	U	S	C	B	V	E
L	N	M	R	S	A	T	O	E	C
U	I	T	E	B	V	E	L	R	O
E	C	H	O	L	E	R	A	L	L
E	H	A	T	I	L	I	L	L	I
S	I	H	O	P	L	A	G	U	E
H	E	A	D	L	I	C	E	Y	O

(Answers on page 186.)

Bugs by Numbers

Here is the big, the small, the mega, the minuscule, the long and the short of the bug world:

5,000,000,000,000,000,000,000,000,000,000
Roughly the total number of bacteria living on the Earth.

3,500,000,000
Roughly the number of years that bacteria have lived on the Earth.

1,000,000
Number of people that 1 gram of the toxin made by the *Clostridium botulinum* bacteria could kill.

1,000+
Number of soccer pitches covered by a type of fungus that some scientists think is the world's largest living organism.

40
Percentage of the adult population of the African country Swaziland that is infected with the life-threatening virus HIV.

30
Number of seconds between each death of a child in Africa from the mosquito-spread illness malaria.

25
Percentage of all the deaths in the world that are caused by infectious diseases due to bugs like bacteria and viruses.

15
Number of seconds between each death in the world caused by the tuberculosis bacteria.

10

Length in metres of the beef tapeworm that can live in our guts.

1

Weight in kilograms of all the bugs in our guts.

0.0000001

Metres across from one end to the other of a rotavirus that gives kids diarrhoea.

0.00000000001

Weight in grams of an *E. coli* bacteria.

Answers to puzzles

PUZZLES TO BUG YOUR BRAIN #1: THE RIDDLE OF THE SANDS
ANSWER: Jigger

PUZZLES TO BUG YOUR BRAIN #2: THE DA BACTERIA CODE
ANSWER:

This poor girl has a fever and a really bad skin rash over her tummy, arms and legs, plus lots of other nasty symptoms. She has toxic shock syndrome caused by *Staphylococcus aureus* bacteria. She needs medicines called antibiotics.

PUZZLES TO BUG YOUR BRAIN #3: SCRAMBLED BUGS
ANSWERS: 1. Warts   2. Fever   3. Jigger   4. Tapeworm   5. Virus   6. Gangrene   7. Fungus   8. House dust mite   9. Guinea worm   10. Sleeping sickness.

PUZZLES TO BUG YOUR BRAIN #4: ENTER THE MICROBIAL MATRIX

A	S	H	I	V	E	R	A	Q	U
L	H	I	N	I	T	B	N	F	N
M	A	L	A	R	I	A	E	E	R
F	U	N	G	U	S	C	B	V	E
L	N	M	R	S	A	T	O	E	C
U	I	T	E	B	V	E	L	R	O
E	C	H	O	L	E	R	A	L	L
E	H	A	T	I	L	I	L	L	I
S	I	H	O	P	L	A	G	U	E
H	E	A	D	L	I	C	E	Y	O